THIS BOOK can't make you a star. Only your talent, professionalism and perseverance can do that. These pages do, however, pass along a great deal of information that can help you reach your goals faster and with less hassle. By reading this book you can get your voice-over career started right away, no matter where you live and no matter what you sound like.

You'll be amazed at how much money a voice talent can make. You may also be amazed at how little they can make. This book will either convince you to follow your dreams to vocal stardom, or to stay out of show business. It is honest and straightforward.

It is not my intention to lead you on with promises, take advantage of your enthusiasm or cash in on any inexperience. I want you to know the ins and outs of the business, as well as a few tricks-of-the-trade so you can make a wise decision about a voice-over career.

And you know what? A lot of us think it's a terrific career. It's like make-believe with a paycheck. If you can stand it, you'll love it. And, in the end, if you decide this is not the career for you, then we will have obtained success there as well. You see, the voice business doesn't need more people. It does need exciting new talent with interesting voices and brains in their head. You may be one of them. You may not. One thing's for sure, by the time you finish this book, you'll know.

CHRIS DOUTHITT

D1113809

This book is available through bookstores or, for fastest delivery, direct from the publisher by calling 1-800-557-3378. Discounts are available for classes. Please write publisher for details.

Published by
GREY HERON BOOKS
P.O. Box 69552
Portland, Oregon 97201

Printed in the United States of America
Book design by The Felt Hat
Photo credits: *page 44, 78, 90, 176 – Roger Douthitt; page 208, 130 – Tom Wiecks; page 231 – Paul Wooley*

PUBLISHER'S CATALOGING IN PUBLICATION
prepared by Quality Books, Inc.

Douthitt, Chris
    Voice-overs : putting your mouth where the money is /
by Chris Douthitt ; edited by Tom Wiecks.
    p. cm.
    Includes index.
    Preassigned LCCN: 96-77899
    ISBN 0-935566-21-X
    1. Voice-overs – Vocational guidance. 2. Radio Announcing – Vocational Guidance. 3. Television Announcing – Vocational guidance. I. Title
PN1990.9.A54D68 1996   791.44'028'023
                              QBI96-40569

Voice-Overs:
Putting Your Mouth
Where the Money Is

BY

Chris Douthitt

EDITED BY

Tom Wiecks

Acknowledgments

Johnny and JoAnn Gunn, Terry Walker, Bob Lloyd,
Gloria Hobson, Jack Angel, Joan Ellen Gerber, Kathy and
Pete Randall, Vicky Vose, Todd Tolces, Michele Mariana,
Mary McDonald-Lewis, Russ Fast, Jackie Hallock,
Michael Carter, Lindsey McGill, Russ Gorsline,
Rob Perkins, Jo Dunbar, Nurmi Husa, Lester B. Hanson,
Dave Mathew, Robert Carlson, Al "The Pal", Ed Collier,
Brian Mount, Professor Irv Broughton, BAMM,
Stuart Pemble-Belkin, William Woodson, Janet Barrett,
Marianne Doherty, Jim Baer, Gary and Debbie Fine,
Mom, Dad, Big B., Clyde and C.J. are just some of the
special people who have shared their talents, wisdom and
friendship with me. Thank you all.

Dedicated to Carol,
the only voice I love hearing every day

Caution: Disclaimer

This book's goal is to provide an overview of the voice-over business to those who may have an interest in pursuing it. It is offered with the understanding that neither the author nor the publisher are rendering legal, accounting or other professional services. When required, such expert assistance should be sought from competent professionals.

Success in the voice-over business is not a sure thing. While some voice-over performers earn large sums of money, others do not. A voice-over career is not a plan for getting rich quick. It can require a significant investment in both time and money, and the author and publisher can offer no guarantees of success.

The book is as complete and accurate as we could make it. Still, no one book can answer every question for everyone, and there may be typographical or other mistakes in this text. Therefore, the author and publisher encourage readers to use this book as a general guide and not to regard it as the ultimate source of information on a voice-over career. Readers should explore other books on the subject as well, and be aware that the information presented here may not be accurate because of developments occurring after our printing date.

The author and Grey Heron Books shall not be responsible or liable to any person or entity for any loss or damage caused, or alleged to be caused, by the information given in this book. *Readers who do not wish to be subject to this disclaimer may return the book to the publisher. Their money will be refunded.*

Contents

Preface

VICKY WAS BORN TALENTED. From her first breath, she was destined for show business and, sure enough, when Vicky grew up she sang on the stage, danced on national television and acted on the big screen. Mostly, however, Vicky talks. Out loud. Into a microphone. And sells everything from auto parts to salsa with her voice. For though she is a multifaceted performer, Vicky's biggest show biz pleasure is commercial voice acting, developing characters, exploring emotions and offering insight by exercising a highly skilled union of mind and mouth. She loves it, and listeners can tell.

Vicky is one of thousands of voice talents populating our airwaves. From the outside, it's hard to tell just where her talent comes from. She's college educated, 4'10" tall with curly hair. She lives in the Pacific Northwest, exercises regularly and makes award-winning fudge.

Oh sure, she probably has some special talent genes courtesy of some distant ancestor, but at the heart of this skilled and confident professional are many years of diligence, determination and dedication. Vicky works now, doing what she loves, because she worked to get here.

That's what this book is about. Not about *this* Vicky in particular, but about all the other Vickys and Victors just dying to tell us which car to drive, which sneakers to purchase, which candidate to trust or which airline to fly. Commercial voice actors are a special breed, and though they may complain about the cost, the competition and the often crazy nature of the industry, I don't know anyone who wants out.

This book looks at voice work from the *outside*. There are other good books on the market that take an actor's perspective, but here we will take a producer's-eye view of talent. You'll find out what is expected of you by the writer, studio engineer, advertising agency, talent agent, actors' union, your fellow performers and, of course, the client. You'll learn all the skills necessary to become a professional voice talent except one: *How To Be Talented*. We will, however, help you find places to develop these skills and hone your performance.

As you peruse the following pages, you will gain insight into the *business* of voice acting. We'll take you from microphone technique to demo tapes, from attitude and agents to an encounter with time and back again. Oh yes, we'll also try to make it fun. This is one course where talking in class is encouraged.

CHAPTER I

The Perfect Voice

The morning air was so crisp it surprised my skin. The sun still explored the horizon, deciding whether to rise, and crickets sang repetitive tones in the brush. I slipped the key into the ignition of my new Conquistador LX30, clutched the wheel and released 200 horses from their slumber. Just knowing I could do zero to sixty in 7.2 seconds was excitement enough. The Conquistador LX30 — excitement comes standard.

OKAY. Before we go any further, go back and read that opening paragraph again. Only this time, read it out loud. Depending on where you are at the moment, this might be embarrassing, but you're never going to be a top voice talent reading to yourself. So, without any direction, just give it a shot, as if you were the actor in front of the microphone chosen to do this 30 second spot. We'll meet again on the next page.

Now go back over it again. This time change the emphasis words. For instance if you emphasized the word *crisp* in the first line last time, now put the emphasis on *air* or *morning*. Go through the whole spot, purposely changing your first impression, and see how different the read can be. If you don't remember what you did last time, you'll need to pay better attention to yourself. Good voice talents are always in control of their instruments. Go for it. I'll wait.

DID YOU NOTICE that you could virtually put the emphasis on any word? As you change the importance of words, the meaning of the sentence can also change. By stress, volume, speed, vocal quality and emotion, you control the sound of the words and thereby the "feeling" of the commercial.

Now, go back and read the first paragraph once again. You're probably wondering if you'll ever get off page one, but never fear. We'll move ahead soon. There's an adage in the business that you will do seven "takes" for every director in the room. Anyway, read it again and this time twice as fast. Don't lose any of the emphasis or emotion. Therein lies the challenge.

HOW'D YOU DO? You may wish to read it a couple more times using a stopwatch just to get a better feeling for time. This script is written to be read in 30 seconds. Did you notice how time constraints affect performance? Did you find yourself changing the emphasis and phrasing to accommodate breathing? Was breath control a problem? Did you skip words or lose your place in the copy? How was your eye-to-mouth coordination?

Hopefully, these are all exciting new experiences for you. We've just covered three basics of voice-over:

1. Reading out loud
2. Reading for emphasis
3. Reading for time

Once you master these basics you'll be on your way to the financial and emotional rewards of commercial voice acting. Well, actually, there are a few other things you might like to know before embarking on your career. That's what the rest of the book is about.

There are a handful of real rules to observe and many unwritten ones I'll attempt to put into writing. Mastering these techniques is critical to success because your goal in this business is to get regular work. In most professions, getting a job is the end. In voice acting, getting a job is just the first major step. It's getting a job on a regular basis that potentially makes you wealthy in both spirit and wallet.

As in most acting, there are rewards in the performance itself. Performing with others, adding a vocal twinkle at just the right place, getting the writer to laugh out loud — all are rewards actors know well. They do not, however, pay the bills. Successful voice actors can live comfortably. They can even get rich. But you must understand that the vast majority merely eke out a living, or they supplement their voice career with a "regular" job. This is true in all markets regardless of size. So simply choosing to start in a big money market does not necessarily improve your chances.

You're probably reading this book because one or more of the following conditions apply:

- People have told you that you have an interesting voice.
- You've heard people doing voices in commercials and you think you can do it.
- You think it's an easy way to make money.
- You're a stage, radio, TV performer or model looking to add versatility and dimension to your career.
- You have a friend who does voice work.
- You think it might be a fun profession.
- You're a born show-off, and you've been doing funny voices since you could speak.

All of these conditions are good reasons to start a career in voice acting. You will need to meet many other conditions, however, in order to continue your career.

Where does talent come from? Let's get some semantics out of the way. The word "talent" as used in this book can mean two things: the actor (anyone who stands in front of a microphone or a camera is referred to as "the talent", whether they deserve the title or not), or the natural or learned abilities of that actor. In other words, a talent has talent. Or at least we hope so!

Let's talk about where talent, the person, comes from. Talent comes from anywhere and everywhere. The major entertainment centers don't have a monopoly on talent. Talent comes from Cleveland, Ohio, from Eugene, Oregon; Ojai, California; Grand Rapids, Michigan; Falls Church, Virginia; Patna, India and thousands of cities around the world.

In fact, most professional voice talent have been many places and tried many careers. The major markets tend to attract those who have garnered some success in their home towns. Some beginning voice talent may find it easier to pursue their career in, say New York or Los Angeles because the systems are all in place: agents, casting services, classes, workshops and an overabundance of studios and production companies. But remember, as the volume of available work increases, so does the volume of competition. In the larger markets you tend to compete with the top talent from the smaller markets who have all come to the big city to make it bigger.

The best advice is to start your career wherever you happen to be at the moment. Find any outlet that gives you the opportunity to read aloud. Possibly there are oral interpretation classes available in your area. Maybe you can find reading groups for poetry or Shakespeare. Get into community theater or try "open mike" stand-up comedy. Your city may need volunteer radio readers for the blind or storytellers for schools and daycare. Harder to get will be the jobs in radio or television, but they are well worth the effort. Call local recording studios or talent agents to see if voice classes are taught by local professionals. If all else fails, get yourself a tape recorder and read anything into it. Practice using your vocal instrument.

Also, get used to hearing yourself played back. Nearly everyone's reaction to hearing their voice is cringing dissatisfaction. You're used to hearing yourself not only through your ears, but through your bones as well! You usually sound warmer and more resonant to yourself than to others, or to a microphone. Start learning your own voice and how to manipulate it.

That brings up the second definition of "talent." There's a lot to be said for the idea that talent is something you're born with. It is equally true that many people can be educated and trained to develop talent — sometimes by extensive practice, other times by discovering unrecognized and untapped abilities.

Some professionals will tell you that they perform because they "have to." Not to make ends meet, but because something inside them requires speaking, dancing, singing, playing the piano, or falling from a five story building into an air bag. Without being able to perform, no matter how small the audience, these people are unfulfilled. There are others who seem to be able to turn their talents on and off like a light switch, performing by circumstance rather than inner drive. Both the driven and the on/off types can feel comfortable doing commercial voice work.

Keep in mind that people who are quite talented in one discipline may not be any good at all in another. Even the best mimes, for instance, have no future in radio.

Let's talk about when to get started. You must wait until you have two items well under control: a reasonable grasp of your abilities and a stash of ready cash. This is like starting your own business with you as the product. Depending on where you start and how far you want to go, this career is going to cost you. This book has already set you back a few dollars. (Money well spent, however.) And this is just the beginning! In the smaller markets you'd better have $1,000 to $2,000 of spendable cash available to get your career off the ground. In the major markets the figures may be at least twice this much. The money is to cover the costs of demo tapes, box labels, duplication, head sheets, acting classes, résumés, union fees and most important, the second edition of this book, whenever it's published. All this is money over and above your normal living expenses.

The recording business is cyclical. It experiences slow times, usually during the summer and early winter.

At these times, competition is high for the little work available. The pro talent tend to use slow periods to get their sales materials in order, revise their tapes and mail greetings. You may be better off getting your schtick together when the competition isn't so active. On the other hand, since business is slow, producers may have more time to listen to new talent, even though they may not have any work to give you. Either way, it's a gamble that you'll hit the right person on the right day. The best bet is to go when you are ready.

Now let's listen to your voice and see if it meets the criteria of the "perfect" voice. Do you speak clearly? We're not talking about precision here, we just want to understand you. Do you have any speech problems such as lisping (thick "S" sound), sibilance (whistling "S" sound), or noisy dentures? If so, you may wish to consult a speech therapist before continuing. Do you have a natural accent? This can help and hurt you. If you can't learn to read without your accent, you will only be cast when that accent is required. This limits your work potential. However, depending on the competition, you may get all the work in your category, which may be significant. All in all, you should probably work on losing the accent. Now you may say, "Everyone has some accent!" That's true, but as a general rule the commercial world tends to prefer voices that are not firmly typed to a particular region.

Do you have good breath control? If you suffer from respiratory problems, you may wish to reconsider this career. If you just need to learn proper breathing and control, look into taking some speech or acting classes.

Is your normal speaking voice interesting? Does it have

some character? Is it raspy, resonant, nasal, breathy, cute, powerful, whiny, sophisticated, or monotone? Does it break when you talk? Does it attract attention? If any of these qualities apply, you may be in luck, because producers want voices with character. They want something interesting to catch a listener's ear.

One of the biggest misconceptions of this business is that you need to sound like an announcer to succeed. This notion is far from reality. A special vocal character that sets you apart from the crowd is your best asset. Let's be clear that character is something you have, not something you do.

Does your voice have range? This is not critical, but the bigger your vocal range, the more spots you can work in. For instance, can you provide the voice of a plumber? A butler or maid? A motorcycle gang member? A Saint Bernard? A parakeet? A doormat? A balloon? If you can, you have range. Be careful. Many people believe they have range, but their gang member and their parakeet sound pretty much the same. It's like the impressionist who does a hundred celebrity voices, all of which sound sort of like John Wayne. It's best to get some outside input on how versatile your voice really is.

In the same realm as range is dynamics. Can you whisper in character? Can you shout? Can you convey emotions by varying your volume? Try it.

If you don't feel that you have "the perfect voice," don't give up yet. There are really no rules. The day one producer tells you you're no good, another producer will say you're unique and original. Only after everyone tells you thanks, but no thanks, should you look for another career.

CHAPTER 2

Radio — a Medium for Your Mouth

THERE WAS A TIME, before television, when radio was king. The air was filled with hard-boiled private eyes, valiant attorneys, wise-cracking teachers, crusading reporters, quick-drawing cowpokes, confused adolescents, salty sea captains, fearless space cadets, super superheroes and diabolical denizens of the dark. Known as the Golden Age of Radio, this was the heyday of voice actors. Casting opportunities were diverse, the talent was top-notch and, because they were operating in the *Theater-of-the-Mind*, nothing was impossible. A man could become a werewolf, a woman could go skiing in the Swiss Alps, and a boy could fall in the river and be rescued at the last minute by his faithful dog all without leaving the voice booth. They tapped into an incredible resource: *imagination*. And played it to the hilt. Most of the best voice acting of all time is still to be found in recordings of vintage radio. Do yourself a favor and find some of these recordings. Listen how the actors used timing, characterization, mike presence and vocal control to create pictures in your mind.

During the Golden Age, the most popular and respected actors of the day did radio. Nearly every best-selling book and motion picture was also presented over the audio airwaves. Several radio performers became big stars who later went on to do movies and television. Some of the most enduring characters in history and some of the most memorable moments of drama and comedy are still with us because radio brought them to life.

Today, not many people grow up wanting to be radio actors. Radio is different. The medium itself has not changed, but our perception of it has. Television has taken over the role radio used to play and radio has moved on to become a background medium. We don't really sit down and listen to radio anymore. We just turn it on and let it fill in the gaps as we go about our lives. With a few isolated exceptions, radio theater is a thing of the past. Perhaps the only real link we have to our radio past is in its commercials. Our thirty and sixty second dramatizations of cold and flu symptoms, hazardous driving conditions and indecision over cat food are the last venues for the audio performer. Characters are still developed, roles are cast, scenes are set, and a miniature version of the Golden Age comes to life in the mind of the listener. The same characters that populated the radio stage for three decades can still be heard in this condensed version. In fact, spot writers today tend to use some of the more well-established characterizations of the past to help speed up the recognition process in the listener. In other words, if you use a cliché, you don't have to take time to explain it.

There's one big difference between the way it was done then and the way it's done now. During radio theater's heyday, voice actors would rehearse a script and perform it live, much like a stage play. Today, there are no rehearsals, as such. The talent performs the script several times and the best parts of each performance are assembled into a composite. In some ways, this is an advantage for modern voice actors. They don't have to worry about getting the script down in one perfect read. They can do pick-ups, wild lines (if you're thinking, "Huh?", see the glossary in back), or they can just read the whole thing over. Through editing, the engineer has the ability to cut and paste the various pieces together, so the listener assumes it was all done live.

The modern voice-over talent can also spend more time honing a performance, working on it line by line if necessary. Any gaffe, blunder or blooper is now left on the cutting room floor instead of being broadcast immediately to the masses. The actors of the Golden Age didn't have this luxury. When the red light went on, they had to get it right, and quite commendably, they usually did. This is not to say that they were better actors in the old days. They were simply adapting to their own circumstances. If they had had modern recording equipment, they would have used it. They practiced a specialized craft and had the opportunity to use it on a regular basis. They also had other well-trained radio actors to work with. Modern voice actors have no shortage of talent. They just ply their trade in a different form of radio.

However, there is a growing feeling among many producers, engineers and casting directors that some talent of today have come to use technology as a crutch. "Far too many take a slovenly approach and get away with it," says one casting director. "Their attitude is too cavalier and unfocused. The true pro gets right down to it and concentrates. Everyone should strive for terrific complete reads and not depend on some computer to make them competitive or effective."

Radio acting is unique in that everything about your character must be communicated through your voice. Such things as age, attitude, location, heritage, education, health and social status must be reflected in your vocal character. A very good professional voice talent once called it "acting to a blind audience." To accomplish this, talent will often do a little overacting for radio spots. This is quite acceptable as long as it helps communicate some of the missing visual elements. By the time you add the "hype" factor that is so prevalent in radio advertising, you'll find much of commercial voice acting is commercial voice overacting.

Just like the writers we mentioned above, talent tends to fall back on the old standby cliché voices that have worked in the past and communicate character rather quickly. Opting for the easy characterization, today's talent often use Jack Webb's cop, Howard Duff's detective, Eve Arden's sarcastic schoolmarm, Jim and Mary Jordan's married couple, Janet Waldo's teenager, Gale Gordon's boss, Virginia Payne's kindly mother, Don Ameche and Francis Langford's bickering husband and wife, Ed Gardner's bartender and Mel Blanc's everything else. If the names aren't familiar to you, their characters are. These vocal prototypes have been preserved, in part, by a series of commercial actors recalling and interpreting the originals.

Radio — A Medium for Your Mouth

Stereotypes work well in radio advertising, so it's sometimes surprising when a writer creates a unique character. Writing and performing against type can be dangerous. The unexpected sound may cause a listener to focus too strongly on the character and miss the message, or create a sense of unreality or unbelievability. However, it can also provide the "hook" that cuts through the radio cacophony and draws attention to the spot. It may create a new identity for the product and a new standard in radio characters.

Radio is a unique medium. The single sense aspect of radio makes it the prime proving ground for voice-over.

Voice for television may not seem different at the time of recording, but it is profoundly different in the way it communicates. A melding of picture and sound is critical to the success of television. The video and audio elements must share attitude, style and texture.

Those of us in the audio biz think that sound is the most important aspect of television advertising. Here's our rationalization. For a brief moment, the TV set goes to black between programs and commercials. In this blink of an eye, the viewer's attention is often diverted from the screen. Without an abrupt, unusual, attention grabbing sound to pull the viewer back, many TV spots never get noticed. The picture is locked into its nineteen-inch-diagonal frame and can't get out. Sound, however, fills the room and grabs at even passive ears. Video people dispute this of course, and with the advent of the remote MUTE button, the best sound in the world may not get the chance to do its job.

Radio has no alternative but to appeal to the ears. There's no second chance. Human beings have a great ability to "tune out" unpleasant sound, so it's obvious that everything you say and how you say it makes a big difference in whether the spot works or not.

Perhaps it's a bit harder on modern voice actors. They actually have to get the listener's attention before they can communicate. The actors of the Golden Age had an eager and attentive audience hanging on every word. But whether it was Orson Welles and The Mercury Theater convincing Americans that they were engaged in a war with Mars, or somebody like you convincing working women to buy a new brand of deodorant, it's a rare and special profession, where the power of the spoken word is put to use in its natural environment.

CHAPTER 3

For What It's Worth

Money isn't everything —
but it's sure ahead of whatever is in second place.

WHEN YOU'RE WORKING in the studio, it's entirely possible for you to make over a thousand dollars per minute as a voice talent. Most often, however, you will earn about two dollars per minute. Either way, it's good money — if you can earn it consistently.

How much you can make will depend on several factors. The size of your market is generally the primary factor. For the most part we'll be talking about small to medium size markets here. The major markets can be so different that they distort the averages. If the talent union is not active in your area, there may not be a printed rate sheet available. Other actors may be of assistance on what the going rate is for your city. You may have to make an offer or negotiate a price with the producer. It is important that you place a good value on your talents. Do not give them away, except as a donation to a worthy cause.

Remember that the client is using your abilities to make money. You are applying your skills, training and good name to the product. Don't sell yourself short.

The important thing here is consistency. Don't charge varying rates to various producers. It's best to set a price and stick to it. Either charge per hour or per project. Voice-over for television usually pays more than radio. Long format narration pays even more. A spot airing locally should cost less than a spot airing regionally or nationally. The product itself should have no effect on your rate. You don't charge a hospital more than the corner drugstore just because they're bigger. Whether you think of your voice as a loaf of bread or a Rolls Royce, it must have worth. The price tag you place on it should be a fair representation of your ability and the value it provides to the finished product. In most cases, the talent fee is one of the least expensive components of advertising. Creative fees, post production and the purchase of airtime can all cost more than you, so make sure you get your share. This is not meant as an endorsement of greed. Actors, as a whole, are noted for their selfless devotion to their craft — the words "starving" and "actor" have long been linked. Putting a price on your talents is not a sell-out. It is simply an acknowledgment of your self worth.

If you live in a city where the talent union is firmly established, a published set of rates will be in effect. Union rates are established by negotiations between the union and producers, on both a national and a local level. National rates usually apply for non-broadcast productions and broadcast spots airing outside your local's jurisdiction. The union local negotiates with local producers to set rates in keeping with the region's production demands and economic conditions. In other words, they are based on what the market will bear.

Another factor that will determine your rate will be your abilities. If you are highly talented and have consistently proven your excellence in performance and efficiency, you may be able to demand more money for your services. Even if you work under a union contract, you may charge more than the union minimum. This is called working for "over scale." Some people add to their rate by percentage, such as charging 150% of scale. Others simply charge double or even triple scale. You have to be pretty sure of yourself to raise your rates.

Some talent make the mistake of demanding special compensation while leaving the producer unsatisfied with their performance. Nothing kills a long-term working relationship faster than making the producer feel she's paid too much for too little. On the other hand, there are many talent who are a bargain at twice the price. Their versatility, ability to take direction, professionalism and credibility exceeds the producer's expectations while saving both time and money. Most producers don't mind paying extra for that kind of peace of mind.

Your talent agent can affect your rate. An effective and aggressive agent who is enamored of your abilities may insist that producers pay a premium for your services. If the agent can wheel and deal more cash for your performance, you both win, since agents make ten percent on top of what you make. It's part of the agent's job to market you for maximum profit. Just remember that you still have to deliver the product they're selling, and you will have the ultimate responsibility of keeping the customer satisfied.

Your rate may also be dictated by competition. If you

offer a unique talent that producers find hard to replace, you may get away with a premium price. If, however, you must compete head-on with several other talent, you'd better stay price-competitive as well.

An extremely busy talent may wish to raise his rate to reduce his workload or to cut down on the risk of over exposure. He may want his rate to reflect his experience or reputation. He may just want the wonderful feeling and prestige of being an over-scale actor, though being an out-of-work over-scale actor is pretty much the same as being an out-of-work scale actor.

Celebrity is also a rate factor. If your voice and name carry unique significance, you can probably put a higher price tag on it. Some celebrity spokespeople are making deals worth millions of dollars for the use of their voice. The implied endorsement of their product by the celebrity is what the advertiser is looking for and they should be prepared to pay dearly for it.

The one thing you shouldn't do is put yourself on sale. Cutting deals can work against you in the long run. To reiterate, being wishy-washy about your price makes a producer question your worth, so don't play money games. If you're a union member, cutting your rate is a violation of your agreement and can get you fined as well as produce resentment on the part of your fellow actors. Developing a reputation as a "bargain basement" voice talent may inhibit your future growth and establish you as someone who will always work for less. It's much better to make yourself worthy of a good price and stick with it.

In the major market of Los Angeles, the going rate is usually over-scale. The flat fee that many agents quote is a combination of union requirements, big city inflation and supply-and-demand principles. For instance, they may say that a radio voice-over is three hundred and twenty-five bucks no matter where it plays — plus the ten percent for the agent, of course. This over-scale pricing doesn't seem to be as prevalent in the other major markets.

Whatever your rate is, know it well, and make sure your producer knows it, too. You don't want any unpleasant scenes after the session. On those occasions when you're in and out of the studio in under fifteen minutes, you may feel uncomfortable or embarrassed to present your bill. Don't be. Think about the studio time you've just saved by being efficient. Think about the investment you've made in preparing for your career. Think about the time and the money you've spent to get yourself to the studio in the first place. Think about taxes and house payments and electric bills. Suddenly, your invoice won't seem that big anymore.

So, just how much are we talking about here? Well, according to 1999 union guidelines (at presstime, negotiations for 2000 are still ongoing), $135.00 to $225.00 for a local radio spot is about average. A local TV voice-over is between $225.00 and $375.00. A six-minute video narration runs about $380.00. These figures are based on thirteen-week use cycles for broadcast and an unlimited "in-house" run for the narration. If the video is to be sold commercially to the public however, the narration rate increases. A voice track on a national TV ad can be worth tens of thousands of dollars, thanks to something called "residuals" which continue paying as long as the spot runs. Being the voice of an animated character on a Saturday morning cartoon show can pay thousands. A spokesperson in a national radio spot can pocket a few grand, too. As we mentioned earlier, Los Angeles rates are usually higher. Figures like these are what keep many voice actors going. The dream of landing the big bucks is an exciting motivation.

Only a small percentage of the available talent ever see their dreams come true, but that doesn't stop thousands of new people from diving into the voice pool every year. The potential monetary returns run from mediocre to Holy Cow! They may help you pay the baby-sitter or they may build you a house. Entering the voice-over business to become rich is a risky venture. But starting a voice-over career because you love it gives you a better chance at getting rich in more ways than one.

Donating your acting services to worthwhile causes and non-profit organizations is a nice way of using your talents. Along with the good feelings it brings, you can also benefit from the exposure, practice and opportunity to make a difference. Public-service spots are often some of the best written, emotion-charged and dramatic spots on the air. If you have established vocal worth, you feel you're giving something of real value while the recipient feels they are getting a truly special gift. If you belong to the union, remember that you must first get a waiver from the union before donating your voice. Also, be sure you fully understand the cause or organization before volunteering. As a media spokesperson, you'll need to share the same goals and point-of-view as the organization for which you are speaking.

Let's talk for a moment about "spec" work. Spec (short for *speculative*) jobs are entered into with full knowledge that there will be no money up-front. Any money will come from future sales. In other words, you are acting as a partial investor, investing your talent and talent fees in a project that could possibly pay dividends in the future.

For What It's Worth

The potential rewards have to be worth more than
the investment, so spec projects are usually accompanied
by lots of exciting promises and hoopla. Approach all
spec jobs with caution. They're not all bad, but a majority
of them never amount to anything. Voice talent are prime
targets for spec projects because it doesn't outwardly
seem that they're giving much away. Talent themselves
often consider their contribution to be easy and not
worth much. Once again, let's push that self-worth button
and remind ourselves about the value of talent. A well-
organized, well-financed venture shouldn't have to ask for
free voice talent, so look it over carefully. Unless you
can see potential for direct benefit, you'd best keep your
distance. If you find a spec project you really want to
get involved in, make sure your effort does not go uncom-
pensated. You're entitled to a good share of the proceeds
if the project succeeds. In most cases, you'll never get
anything for taking the gamble so why not insist that the
payoff be worth the risk? The A.F.T.R.A. talent union
has no provisions for spec performing. If you're a union
member, check with the local office before getting
involved in any speculative project.

A VERSE ON SPEC

If you're asked to work for "spec",
And there's no sign of a check
In the mail.
Then before you start your mission,
Please inspect this definition
In detail.
'Cuz you're asked to take a vow,
That you'll work for nothing now,
Whereupon.
You are promised for your nerve,
You'll get more than you deserve
Later on.

So you work your bloomin' tail
Off for glory, not for scale.
Or for pay.
While your mind is contemplating,
All the wealth that sits there waiting
One fine day.
But when no one gets richer,
And you never seem to get-yer
Just dessert.
Then you'll see, beneath the polish,
"Spec" can also be a smallish
Piece of dirt.

CHAPTER 4

The 4-Point Plan
to Success

THERE MAY NOT BE any hard rules in this business, but there are many guidelines that will help you succeed. Four qualities have emerged that seem to separate the successful professional voice talent from the rest of the world. Stated simply:

1. Competitive abilities
2. Proof of abilities
3. Connection to the work
4. Availability

COMPETITIVE ABILITIES means that you must be at least as good as the people who are already doing the work. With only so much work to go around, producers will always go to the talent they trust. Why should they settle for marginal abilities when there are lots of good alternatives available? You're never going to win a job over someone who is better than you, so you must bring your talent level at least up to the level of your competition. Who is your competition? Just listen to radio and TV commercials. In summary, point one is HAVE TALENT.

PROOF OF ABILITIES is a demo tape. Only a foolish producer would hire a voice based on a written résumé. The only way for you to prove you can read and interpret copy is to perform it on tape for the producer to hear. The standard of the industry is the personal demo. It's your showcase and we'll be devoting a whole chapter to it later.

CONNECTION WITH THE WORK means that you must have some way of knowing when work is available. In smaller markets you may be able to manage this yourself through networking. For most markets, however, you will need help. That help is called an agent. Talent agents are a diverse lot with an often undeserved bad reputation. We'll devote a chapter to agents as well, but suffice it to say that agents can be the catalysts for bringing producers and talent together. That connection is critical to your success.

AVAILABILITY can be the toughest condition of all. No matter how talented you are, no matter how good your tape and how efficient your agent, if you can't make the recording session at 2:40 on Wednesday, you won't work. This makes it difficult to hold down a full-time job because it's often necessary to leave for a couple hours during the middle of the day to practice your voice-over craft. Auditioning can also pull you away at odd times and on short notice. Auditioning is an important component in your success but it pays no money and offers no assurances. Are you willing to take time off work and forfeit pay for a chance at making more? Is your employer willing to let you? Of course, when you're doing voice work all the time you won't need a regular job, and therein lies the paradox. To be successful you must be available and to be available you must be successful.

So, in review, to be a top professional voice talent you must be talented with a demo tape to prove it. You must be well known and respected by the people who do the hiring, or you need an agent to act as matchmaker. Finally, you must be available any time you're needed.

Success is measured personally. You may consider yourself successful working two or three times per year, or you may need to work every day to feel fulfilled. It may be measured in dollars or in personal performance. No matter how you interpret success, practicing these guidelines will greatly improve your chances of achieving it.

CHAPTER 5

Getting Talented

T HE PURPOSE of this book is to explain what to do with your voice talent once you have it.

Let's say that you already have a talent for something. You may not know voice acting yet, but let's suppose you're pretty good at rowing a boat. When you take people out on the lake, they're always asking you how you got so coordinated. They can't figure out how to get the oars in sync and they're constantly pulling too hard with one arm so the boat goes around in circles. You probably answer with a variation of one of these lines: "I don't know really, I've always been able to do it," or "This ol' fisherman taught me." Voice talent will give you the same type of answers concerning their abilities. Some of them have been doing voices and playing characters ever since they can remember. Their families may have encouraged them or they may have performed vocal experimentation in private. Others will tell you that formal education by trained professionals and years of practice produced and developed the skills they have today.

We have no control over how fat our vocal chords are, or how they are attached. Our sinus cavities, tongue, lips, and teeth are predetermined. Our upbringing gives us accents, dialects, lingo and speech patterns. If we're blessed with an interesting voice, it's strictly by hereditary chance. If we don't like our voice, it's hard to get a new one. Therefore, a certain amount of what goes into a great voice is laid out in our DNA and our early development.

Another factor is environment. The amount of humidity in the air, the time of day, degree of air pollution and the temperature of the room all affect how we sound. Some people are "morning voices" who produce their best tones before their vocal chords actually warm up. Others have to scream and shout before performing. There are talent who choke up on a dry day or stuff up when the pollen count gets too high. I even knew one talent who swore by a shot of tequila before stepping up to the mike. I was never sure if it actually improved his performance, however.

But what turns one set of vocal chords into an opera diva, another set into a horse race announcer and still another into the spokesperson for Sani-Claws Cat Litter? The answer lies in learning to apply your voice.

There are many vocal traits you can learn to acquire or learn to lose. One of the most obvious is an accent. People with even the strongest regional dialects can learn to speak without them. If you're from the heart of Brooklyn, you can learn to speak like a proper British nobleman, or if you're a short-order cook from Savannah, you can learn to speak like an authority for a major computer company.

You can also learn good breathing techniques and learn to move your voice from your chest to your nose, to your throat or even to your mouth. You can learn better sight reading, comic timing and improvisation. You can expand your tonal range and develop exercises to keep your voice limber and smooth. You can alter your voice with lemon juice, warm water, decongestants and cigarettes.

In other words, you have a great deal of control over your voice and how you use it. If you're not a born talent, you may very well be a reborn talent.

You need the basic raw material: a voice. If you can force air past your vocal chords and produce a sound, you probably have the raw material. You also need the ambition to improve upon it, and you need imagination.

If you want to develop it, you should probably seek out some voice classes. Look for classes taught by working professionals. Be careful of teachers who are too encouraging. The business is tough and you need to trust the instructor to be honest with you.

Also be wary of teachers who talk too much about themselves. Actors are an egotistical bunch (it's an extremely important motivator), but their classes shouldn't be an ego stroking exercise with an endless stream of performance by the instructor. Look for a teacher who listens and makes the class do the talking. After all, that's what you're supposed to be learning.

Beware of anyone who teaches you to read copy by reading it themselves. This is known as giving you "line readings" and it is a poor form of direction because it makes you reliant on someone else's performance rather than interpreting for yourself. It also turns out students who all sound like the instructor instead of individuals.

A good class will spread over many hours. This isn't something you can learn quickly, so make sure you can commit to the schedule, and check to see if there are advanced classes or workshops available to keep you in practice.

When you go to class, bring along your imagination. It's one of the basic components of a great voice talent.

You have to be able to play a fish on a moment's notice. Not just any fish — a Neon Tetra, for goodness sake. Then, halfway through the session, the director decides that another talent will be the Tetra and you need to become an Angelfish. All the time, naturally, you're selling carpeting, house paint or water filters.

It takes imagination and a certain disregard for logic. You need to place your mind in the environment of the copy, coming out only for an occasional direction between takes.

Getting talented takes lots of practice. It also takes understanding friends who don't mind you reading the newspaper aloud, reciting commercials at the dinner table or talking like a fish in the shower.

If this is beginning to sound like too much for a shy person like yourself, don't worry. Most voice talent tend to be somewhat quiet and reserved in their private lives. They have simply learned one other lesson along the way: how and when to turn their shyness off, and their fish on.

Do you want a basic talent test? Okay, but this test is more fun than scientific. Read the following copy line over and over for one whole minute, giving it a different interpretation each time. Count on your fingers or put a check mark on a sheet of paper for each complete read.

Getting Talented

No repeating styles and no changing the copy, please.

All roads lead to Roseland.

Ready for a grade?

over 30 — A potentially exceptional talent with a
   quick imagination.
20 – 30 — Good job. You show true promise.
10 – 20 — Keep practicing and try it again.
under 10 — Maybe you'll be one of those reborn talents.

Did you change the emphasis word? That was good for
5 reads all by itself. Did you shout it? How about whispering? Were you angry? Sexy? Did you chuckle as you read
it? Did you cry? Did you hold your nose once? Did you
hold your tongue? Did you cup your hands over your
mouth or talk into a coffee cup? Any accents? Slow? Fast?

When you think about it, there are probably hundreds
of possible read styles. All of them may not be commer-
cially suitable, but who's to say? The idea is to explore the
bounds of your voice and to get the brain and the voice
working together.

Here's another quick reading and interpretation test.
There is only one way to read the following line so it
makes sense. You can't rearrange the words and you can't
add or subtract words. How fast can you give it the read
it deserves?

Moses was the daughter of the Pharaoh's son.

Some people spot this one right away. Others find it
a real puzzler. At first glance it appears to be an incorrect
statement. It's a good example of how interpretation can
give totally different meaning to the same line.

41

If you haven't figured it out yet, let me explain. Think about the facts. Moses was the son of the Pharaoh's daughter, right? So when you read it aloud, you need to treat the phrase "the daughter of the Pharaoh's" in a somewhat parenthetical way.

Does it make sense now? If not, come back to it later.

One last quick talent test. Read the following thirty second radio spot. You'll have to read it quickly to get it in time. Read it out loud — we don't read to ourselves anymore, remember?

It's Wolcott Fabrics January Clearance Sale! You'll save 15 to 30 percent on quality fabrics throughout the store. Cottons, knits, corduroy, velveteen, satins and fleece, all marked down for this special sale. Save an additional 10 percent by using your Wolcott QuikCard and pay no interest until May 1st. At Wolcott's you'll always find top fabrics from the looms of Pierson & Jameson, Hilltower Mills and Feelbest. We're open til 9:00 PM Monday through Friday, Saturdays til 6:00 and Sundays til 5:00 at the corner of 5th and Washington in downtown Carsonville.

Okay, now go to the next page.

Getting Talented

(No peeking at the previous page, now.)

What was the name of the store?

_____

What was the name of their sale?

_____

How much was the markdown? (in percents)

_____

You could save 10% more by using what?

_____

How late are they open on Thursday?

_____

The store is located at what cross streets?

_____

Three fabric suppliers were mentioned. Can you name them?

_____

This exercise was to test your comprehension of what you've just read. Did you listen to what came out of your mouth? Did you understand the copy, and did you present it in a way that made the commercial communicate? If you can't communicate with yourself, chances are you won't communicate to the listener either.

CHAPTER 6

The Demo Tape

THE DEMO TAPE is your key sales tool for voice work. It is a place to show off your abilities and prove you have the right sound for the producer's project. How do you know what the producer is looking for? On an individual basis you don't know, but you can do some simple research to find out what's popular.

Listen to radio and TV ads currently running in your area. Are there any trends you can distinguish? Are most spots hard sell? Are they conversational? Can you detect any common delivery styles such as sarcastic, urbane, silly, macho, kindly or aloof? Do you hear more men than women or vice-versa? What's the average age of the voices you hear? Ask talent agents or casting agents what vocal types producers are requesting. If you don't have answers to all these questions, don't worry. Your demo will evolve and change as you learn the system.

Here are some guidelines to help you put it together. If you're just starting out, have no agent and are simply testing the waters, you probably shouldn't spend a great deal of time and money on your tape. Make a cassette at home using ad copy gleaned from magazines or transcribed from the radio. Pick a quiet place for recording, away from noises that may make the tape difficult to listen to. Don't leave mistakes or long pauses on the tape. Don't try to be an announcer, just be yourself, but vary the copy so that the listener can get an idea of your range and versatility.

Most important, keep it short. The maximum tape length should be less than three and a half minutes.

Am I really asking you to go to the trouble of making a "cheapo" demo that you will probably have to throw away? Yes. This is the least expensive and least time-consuming thing you'll ever do in your voice-over career. Yet this simple step stops about 75 percent of the people interested in the profession from going any further. Maybe they don't like the sound of their voice on tape. Maybe they can't find the time to put it together. Maybe it's just a passing fancy and their interest wanes. Whatever the reason, the process has a way of weeding out the casual participants from the true professionals. When you get past this step, you join a special and much smaller group of competitors.

When you have your "home-made" demo completed, do some selective distribution. See if any local producers, recording studio engineers, advertising agency copywriters or talent agents will listen to your tape and give you feedback. Let them know it's your first attempt, but don't make apologies for it. Also, give it to friends whose opinion you trust. You may wish to involve family members or co-workers so they can share the initial stages of your new endeavor.

If you have talent, the proof will shine through. If you don't, you will prove it to yourself first, since you are likely to be one of your own toughest critics.

In the major markets, where the level of competition is very high, you'll probably have to skip this step and go directly to making a fully-produced demo.

Some talent have actually gotten work from their home-made demo. Some have used it to land an agent. One of the first things a new agent will probably do is ask you to revise your tape. This is why I told you not to spend too much time and money on the first one.

The next step is to produce your REAL demo, the one destined for the masses. Throughout his or her career, the average talent will go through many revisions of their demo tape, but the first real demo is probably the most important. The first tape a producer or casting agent gets from you may be the only one he or she ever remembers, so it better be a fair and accurate representation of what you can do and how well you can do it.

Here are some thoughts, collected from dozens of industry insiders, that you may wish to keep in mind as you create this important sales tool.

KEEP IT SHORT. A good professional demo tape should be three and a half minutes or less. The idea is to show as much versatility as you can as quickly as you can.

GET A PROFESSIONAL SOUND. Local studios may have special recording deals for new talent. Also, some voice classes include recording time as part of tuition. What you need to get is a high quality reproduction of your voice on tape through the use of a good microphone, a good recorder, a good mix and a good engineer. Cost factors will vary depending on your location and the amount of production involved. Studios usually charge an hourly rate plus the cost of materials. Choose a studio that specializes in commercial production rather than music. These studios are more apt to understand your needs. They may give you access to script files and inside information on agent selection, client prospects and distribution of your tape. The studio may do some voice casting itself, in which case you've made a valuable contact.

GET SOMEONE TO DIRECT your session. Seek out a trained professional and be willing to pay for his or her time. At many studios, the production engineers will provide this service. If this is not possible, bring in an objective friend who will recognize a good read and won't be afraid to critique your performance if necessary. You are not always the best judge of your own work. You'll tend to be overly critical or, conversely, too enamored of your own skills. So get some outside input. Remember, however, that this is your tape and you must be pleased with the final product. You're the one who has to peddle it all over town, so you'd better be proud of it.

START YOUR TAPE with your most normal voice. Assume that no one is going to listen past the first ten seconds. Let's say you can do many different voices and you're particularly proud of an old Russian grandmother character. Because it's so good, you consider putting it first on your tape. The listener only hears the first ten seconds, hears your great Russian dialect, assumes that it's natural and eliminates you from 99 percent of the work. Save the dialects and accents for later in your tape unless, of course, you normally have one. If you simply *must* start with a character voice, make sure your tape label clearly states that you are a "multi-voice."

START WITH A VOICE you can reproduce easily and always start with something you like because it's going to be your vocal signature. You may wish to add a dramatic or ear-catching beginning with music or sound effects. Just remember your time limit. Don't spend a lot of time on anything that isn't you.

THERE IS MUCH DEBATE as to whether personal introductions work on demo tapes. Some people like to say hello, give their phone number, agent's name and warm salutations to the listener. Some people like to explain what they are going to do and others like to ramble on about their life, the business or the difficulty in finding the perfect voice. My favorite phrase about demo tapes comes from the talent agent who said, "Get on with it." Assume that the listener has put your tape into the player to hear you doing ads. Don't delay his or her reward.

TRY NOT TO HIGHLIGHT other people on your tape. Remember that every second they're on, you're not — and you're paying for it. If you do a dialogue sample on your tape (an excellent idea by the way), make sure your counterpart is of the opposite sex and be sure to give yourself all the best lines. I've been surprised by some talent demos where the talent's partner is the key figure of the spot while the demo talent is saying things like, "yeah", "uh huh", "well" and "I see".

As a general unwritten rule, though, a woman should not put other women's voices on her tape. A man shouldn't put other male voices on his tape. It's confusing to the listener and potentially pulls the focus away from you.

GIVE YOUR TAPE A PERSONALITY — preferably your own. If you are bright and cheery with lots of energy and excitement, then your tape should be the same. By contrast, if you tend to be a serious, no-nonsense, straight-talking kind of individual, then your tape should also have these qualities. This can be accomplished mainly through proper copy selection, but other mood setting devices include music, sound effects and pacing.

NO MATTER WHAT pace you set for your tape, keep it moving. Don't leave gaps or long pauses. Cut all the samples tightly together. Don't worry about communicating ideas as much as communicating sounds. Don't do entire radio ads — you don't need sixty seconds of one read style. As one talent put it, "Don't give the listener a chance to turn off the tape". Remember the ten second rule: a listener can make casting decisions in ten seconds or less. If the listener likes what you're doing, ten seconds will be enough time to prove it. If the listener doesn't like what you're doing, you'd better get on to something else. Use sharp cuts and dramatic mood shifts to show off your vocal range. Cutting from the middle of a soft intimate spot for perfume to a raucous read for monster trucks shows acting dynamics and vocal diversity at its best. Avoid long fades in and out of spots. Avoid long instructions or explanations. In short, avoid being dull.

USE NON-COMMERCIAL MATERIAL SPARINGLY, if at all. Your prowess on the Shakespearean stage may be second to none, but filling your tape with soliloquies does not work in your favor. Remember that a vast majority of the time you will be hired to sell something like pretzels, steam irons or a local dry cleaner. If you still choose to do Lady MacBeth, have her do an ad for spot remover. At the very most, restrict her to a couple lines for use as vocal contrast filler. The same applies to poetry readings, story-telling, stand-up comedy routines or speeches. They are all worthy abilities but a commercial voice demo, first and foremost, needs to be commercial. Whatever you do, try to show how your talents can be used in a commercial way.

THERE ARE JOBS THAT REQUIRE specialized vocal abilities such as cartoons, fashion shows, educational nar-ration, telephone or computer voice messages and singing. If you have a particular interest or talent in these areas you may wish to include samples on your demo tape, or you may wish to produce a separate tape for use when these opportunities arise. If you're looking for work as a radio personality, disc jockey, newsperson or sportscaster, you'll need specialized tapes known as "air checks". These are not the same as commercial demos, and they are not interchangeable.

AVOID TOPICAL MATERIAL. Your tape may need to last for quite a while, so stay away from things that date it. Also avoid controversial and political material. Your tape is not the place to expound your beliefs and causes. During your commercial voice career, you may encounter numer-ous occasions when moral decisions will need to be made. Someday you may need to draw the line between selling product and selling out, and you should feel no undue pressure in your decision. You shouldn't, however, lose a job selling furniture just because you put an endorsement for a Democratic candidate on your tape and the client is a Republican. In a perfect world, the client wouldn't make such a biased decision. But the real world is far from per-fect, and you can diminish the potential negative response by not presenting your own biases on your demo.

ARRANGE YOUR SAMPLES for maximum contrast. Cut soft sell to hard sell, conversational to announcer, dialogue to introspective, comic to serious, etc.

KEEP CHARACTERS LIKABLE. Many talent make the mistake of using voices that are unpleasant to hear. Whiny spouses, angry parents, nasty teens, pushy sales-people and bad impersonations can all elicit painful reactions from listeners. If you use these types of char-acters, use them a little at a time.

DON'T STRETCH BEYOND your abilities. Demo tapes can show your limitations just as well as your talents. Don't do voices that are difficult for you to reproduce. Don't use extensive electronic processing such as echo, pitch changing or over-dubbing. Don't vary the speed of your voice electronically. Everyone sounds like an elf when they're sped up so don't bother proving you do, too. If you do celebrity impressions, make sure they are perfect copies or solid characterizations. Otherwise your tape will show where you're good and where you're not so good. Try not to do other people's characters. There will be very little call for your version of Bugs Bunny, Mickey Mouse or Kermit the Frog for both creative and legal reasons.

FOREIGN ACCENTS should be kept to a minimum. Even in the smaller markets, voice talent with authentic accents are usually available. Given a choice, producers will nearly always take the authentic accent over the fake one. The same holds true for adults doing children's voices. Many adults do terrific kid voices, but many kids can do them even better and the number of talented kids is usually more than enough to handle the limited workload. If you do accents or kid voices, relegate them to minor status on your tape. If you intend to specialize in animation voices, you should probably make a separate tape of such characters for producers who specialize in that field.

DEPENDING ON what's standard in your market, your demo could end up in a variety of formats. Audio cassette and ¼" reel-to-reel tape are the most popular while DAT (Digital Audio Tape) and CD (Compact Disc) are making more and more appearances. It's best to talk with local producers or agents to find out what they expect.

WHATEVER FORMAT YOU CHOOSE, make sure your copies are of good quality. You can spend a considerable amount of cash producing your demo only to have it ruined in the duplication phase. Check your dubs (copies) to make sure they run at the right speed. Make sure they're not distorted by over-modulation (too loud) or hard to hear due to under-modulation (too quiet). Check to see that nothing is cut off at the beginning or end, and that there are no unexpected pauses. Make sure any dead space up to the start isn't too long. After hitting PLAY, you shouldn't have to wait any longer than 10 seconds for the tape to start. Your dub should be a reasonable representation of your master tape. It shouldn't be hissy or muddy, faster or slower, wowwy or too quiet. Don't compromise on your dubs, and don't distribute tapes without checking them first.

LABEL YOUR DEMO CLEARLY and completely. During a heavy casting session, tapes can get separated from their boxes, so make it easy for the producer to put them back together by labeling both the box and the tape. Provide all necessary information such as your name and your agent's name and phone number. Optional information such as union affiliation, your personal phone number(s), fax number, vocal age range, title, slogan, tape length, table of contents, brief list of regular clients, reviews or written description of your style can be included, usually on the box label only. Artwork can be added to make your tape visually interesting. If you also do on-camera work, you can add your picture. Also think about how your dub will be stored. Most tapes and CDs are stored on edge, like a book, so it's important to label the edge. This is the part of your box producers will see as they peruse their casting shelf. Once again, present your personality on your label. Are you flashy colors or business suit gray? Are you orderly and distinguished or wild and unpredictable? Is your tape funny? Is it corporate? Is it theatrical? Here is a chance to express yourself both audibly and visually. Give it some careful thought. And don't think you have to spend a lot of money; a tight budget can produce some of the most creative designs. There's a competitive motivation as well. Think about how your tape will stand out from all the other tapes around it.

BOX LABELS can be obtained through many printers. These include adhesive labels for your tape and "J-cards" which are specially designed labels for the cassette box. Talk to your local talent agents or other talent to find out who has the best deal. When laying out your label, keep in mind that things tend to change. Put information such as agent and phone number in a block that can be covered with a small sticker should these details change. That way, you won't have to reprint your entire box label.

DON'T START a demo tape project unless you're ready to finish it. That means getting the tape fully produced, dubbed, labeled and distributed. There's nothing as worthless as a sales tool that sits on your shelf at home. So many talent get into this costly venture and fail to have enough resources or ambition to complete it. It's unknown whether your demo will ever bring you fame and fortune. It's a safe bet, however, that it will be a total waste of money if you start the project and then don't see it through.

WHEN DISTRIBUTING your tape, do it with pride. Be confident without being cocky. Don't ever make excuses or apologies for the tape's quality or your abilities. Producers should look forward to hearing it, so don't give them anything to worry about. In fact, make it convenient for the producer in every way. Present your tape in the correct format and at the right time. Most producers will not be available to sit down with you and listen to your tape. Many would find that an uncomfortable situation where it's difficult to be honest. The fact is, unless a producer is actively casting when you arrive with your tape, there really isn't much he or she can say other than, "Thanks for the tape. We'll call you if anything comes up." You must be prepared to leave your tape permanently, so get plenty of copies. Asking for your tape to be returned is a sure sign you're not a pro.

BE SURE TO GET YOUR TAPE to the right person. For instance, the ad agency president may be in charge, but isn't usually the one making casting decisions. Make a few phone calls and find out who is so you can personally address your packet. There may be several people at an ad agency or production company who regularly cast voice talent, so you may need to leave a separate dub for each. It's important to know where your tape is going so you can follow up later. Ad producers tend to change jobs quite a bit, so make routine checks to be sure your contacts are still where you think they are.

FINALLY, ALWAYS CARRY a copy of your demo tape. You never know when the opportunity to make a sale will present itself. This is especially true if you're attending industry open houses, parties or gatherings, but you might also meet a producer at a restaurant, at a convention, during a concert or on vacation. Even when you've already been cast for a session, you should bring along a copy of your tape. You may have been cast from an audition or from your agent's "house tape", and the producer may have never heard all the things you can do. You might also meet other people at the session who can provide work. The demo tape is your sales tool. It can't sell when it's at home in a shoebox.

CHAPTER 7

The Agent

GROUCHO: *Well, we get ten percent of their salaries.*
   CHICO: *Don't we have to do anything for the money?*
GROUCHO: *No, we're agents.*
   CHICO: *I know, but what do we do?*
GROUCHO: *NOTHING! WE'RE AGENTS!*
   CHICO: *Say, I've been an agent for years.*

THIS SHORT INTERPLAY from the Marx Brothers routine called *Hollywood Agents* is pretty typical of how talent agents have been portrayed in the media. Agents have a reputation of being the bad guys of the industry. Usually they don't deserve it, but when you look at the difficult position they hold, it's somewhat understandable.

An agent's job is to represent the talent's interests in all business dealings. They make their money through a ten-percent commission on everything the talent earns. Sometimes this ten percent is added on top of the talent's fee and sometimes it is deducted from the talent's fee. Because of this arrangement, a talent may look at his agent as sponging off his labor while the customer looks at the agent as adding unnecessary cost to the talent's services. Everyone assumes that the agent isn't working hard enough and makes too much money. Everyone except the agent, that is.

"My agent is a devious, pushy, money grubbin',
gladhandin' con man. In fact, he's the best agent in town."

Actually, many agents earn their ten percent and much
more. They come in all varieties, just like the talent
they represent, and they provide a valuable service to the
media community. Unless an agent represents a small
handful of very busy talent, he must maintain a fairly large
pool of performers within his "stable" in order to survive.
The relative strength of this pool gives the agent credibility in the production arena. The stronger the pool, the
busier the agent. The busier the agent, the more good
talent wish to be part of the pool, which makes it stronger,
which makes the agent busier which...well, you can see
that the relationship between agent and talent is an important one for both sides.

From the producer's standpoint, the agent is a handy
source of talent when needed. With a single phone call
a producer can round up the voices of a grandfather in his
70's, a mom and dad (he a construction worker, she an
investment counselor), an 8-year old with an attitude, and
their family cat — a Seal-Point Siamese. The agent will
gather the talent, hold an audition, make recommendations, distribute demo tapes, quote rates, handle the
scheduling and paperwork and intercede between the
producer and talent if a problem arises. In some cases this
means that the agent must take the heat from both sides
and cool it down with compromise.

"...in accepting this award I want to thank my mother and
father, my husband, whose unerring support has helped
me through the tough times, and I also wish to thank my
agent..."

The Agent

Agents can be crucial to a talent's success, particularly
for talents who have difficulty selling themselves. The
shyest of talents can have a flamboyant agent acting
as their front man. By contrast, an over-enthusiastic and
pushy talent may need a mellow agent to soften the blow.

The agent is available, even when you're not. If you
want to go on vacation, you can leave your agent to deal
with your business affairs. If a job arises, the agent
can talk with the producer personally, weigh the benefits,
negotiate rescheduling, discuss extra fees and call you
for a decision. It's much more efficient than an answering
machine. Also, with an agent you won't have to leave
a forwarding number all over town every time you take a
vacation.

"My agent certainly recognizes talent.
She quit being an actor."

Your agent should be well known, knowledgeable of
the market and involved in the media community.
Agents tend to specialize, so make sure your agent has a
good reputation in commercial voice work. How does
he promote his stable of voice talent? Does he have lots of
demo tapes available in his office? Do you feel comfortable talking with him? Do you think producers will?
Is there a person on staff who specializes in handling
voice talent? Does the agent have space and equipment for
voice auditions? Is he franchised by the talent unions?
Do you detect enthusiasm or resentment toward his
profession and the local producers? These are all questions
you need to ask before signing with a talent agent.

An agent will be asking several questions about you as
well. Agents usually represent a wide variety of talent.

They handle voice talent, on-camera actors, print models, runway models, live performers, singers, musicians, clowns and, sometimes, trained animals. If you can perform in more than one category, you will be more valuable to the agent. Being just a voice talent limits the amount of work you can do in the market. An agent may steer you into TV and print as well as voice to help broaden your marketability. Remember that an agent only gets ten percent of what you make so the more earning potential you have, the more profitable you can be for the agent.

An agent will also want to hear your demo and see if you will be competitive with the rest of the talent pool. She'll want to see if your voice and style conflicts with talent she already represents. She'll want to know about your background, experience, union affiliation and attitude. The agent will probably have recommendations for your demo tape, photo composite and résumé. She may make calls to other talent and producers checking on your reputation. The agent's stable of talent may be so large that she already has difficulty keeping track of everyone. In this case, she may suggest you seek out a smaller operation where you can get more personal attention.

After you sign with an agent, he or she may check on your reliability and performance. Did you make the client happy? It's a sure bet your agent will hear about it if you didn't. If you screw up on the job, your agent, and all the talent he or she represents, stand to lose future work from that client. Likewise, you're likely to hear about screw-ups on the part of your agent.

"Sooner or later, you'll hate your agent."

The Agent

Unfortunately, this comment, made by a successful Los Angeles voice talent, tends to ring true. The show business and commercial production industry is fraught with peril. Strained relationships, hurt feelings, embattled egos, unfair producers, squabbles over payment and performance, deadline pressures, monetary demands, changes in the marketplace, competition and the sometimes illogical decision-making process all contribute to eventual conflicts with your agent. Sometimes these problems can be worked out. Other times they lead to a business divorce. It does neither party any good to be at odds with the other. You have to trust and rely on your agent and your agent must be able to endorse you wholeheartedly. No matter whose fault it is, the situation demands prompt attention before either of you damages the reputation or credibility of the other. At the same time, there are many stories of lifelong talent/agent relationships, tales of mutual respect and mutual success. It's questionable if talent and agents can ever become true friends, for no matter how chummy they become, they must remember that it's business that brings them together.

Talent agents are found in some small markets. They are most prevalent, however, in the bigger cities where the production workload can support them. There may be several in your area. Look in the phone book under *Talent Agencies/Casting Directors*, or call a local recording studio to get names and numbers.

It is unlikely that a talent agent will ever come looking for you, so be prepared to make the first move. Go to your first meeting prepared with a reasonably produced demo tape and a clean résumé of your background and related accomplishments. Bring photos or print material if you wish to do on-camera work. This is business, so dress accordingly.

Be careful not to present a cocky attitude. Remember in our *4 Point Plan to Success* first you have to have the talent, then you have to prove it. Until then, try to be humble. A good agent isn't going to be fooled anyway.

Getting an agent to believe in you is an important initial step. Getting that agent excited about you is even better. They are your link to the work, and you want your name to be on the tip of their tongue when producers call.

It is possible to make it without an agent, especially in the smaller markets, but you will need to be prepared to do all the legwork and all the networking necessary to move your career forward. In the major commercial markets, an agent is mandatory.

'My agent isn't getting me any work."

Let's be clear about one thing. An agent doesn't get you work. Your talents and abilities get you the job. An agent may organize the session, but you are the one who earned it. Even with an agent, you will do much of the work and, in return, will receive most of the accolades and money. When an agent starts believing that he or she is responsible for a talent's success, the system starts to break down. Likewise, when a talent believes that her agent is the real reason she's working or not working, the system experiences the same problems. This is not to say that a good agent doesn't deserve some credit when a job is landed. Sometimes it is the agent's name or reputation that first attracts a producer. The agent is a middleman, a matchmaker if you will, who provides a service for both the producer and the talent. Whether you consider your agent to be an answering service, a promoter, an advisor, a bean counter, a confidant or a con man, you must always remember where the talent lies. Your relationship with your agent is extremely important but, in the end, your successes and your failures will depend mostly on you.

"I know an agent who started opening branch offices overseas. Now his talent is out of work in seventeen countries."

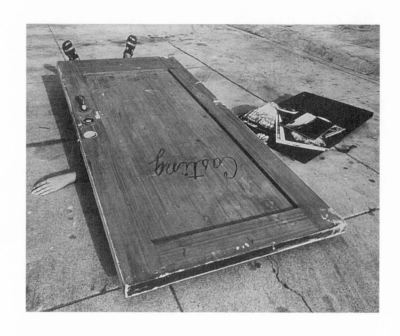

CHAPTER 8

Voice Casting

I'D LIKE TO SAY that casting, on the part of an agency or producer, is a painstaking and logical selection process through which the best person for the job is always hired. I'd like to say that, but it just isn't true. In fact, casting is often a last minute, illogical process through which the best person for the job might possibly get it — maybe. Let me tell you a few casting stories.

There's one about the guy who won a national audition to be the new voice of a company known throughout the world. The ad agency thought he was perfect for all their new TV and radio campaigns and was ready to start recording. Then some executive from the corporation found out that the talent was from a small town on the west coast and decided that their corporate voice should really be someone living in a *big* city. The talent lost the job for residing in the wrong place.

Then there's the one about the two guys who auditioned for a radio commercial that wasn't written very well. They read it once, as written, and then did some careful rewriting to make their characters more interesting and the copy more fun. These two talents didn't make it to the finished spot. But their rewrite did.

You've probably heard about the woman who was cast for a big job simply because she happened to be in the next room when the scheduled talent failed to show up.

And how about the client who directed everyone to try sounding like a popular celebrity during the audition and then ended up hiring the celebrity?

Or the director who hired a talent with an authentic British accent because he "loved his voice" and then, during the session, kept directing him to say things "more American."

And then there was the copywriter who cast his next door neighbor in a spot because he would "sound real." He sounded real, all right. *Real* nervous and *real* stiff. He sounded just like a guy who had never been in a recording studio before. The copywriter learned too late that everybody sounds natural in their natural environment, but it takes an actor to sound real when surrounded by unreality.

Stories such as these are told regularly in the business. They illustrate some common characteristics of casting, characteristics that talent often consider highly unfair. With the exception of a few expert casting directors and skilled production people, the folks involved in casting are often unprepared for the process. Alfred Hitchcock once noted that Walt Disney was the absolute best at casting: "If he didn't like an actor, he could just tear him up."

Voice Casting

Actually, many an actor has been torn from contention before the audition. What follows is a phone conversation between a producer and a studio engineer. The producer, Hal, has called his regular engineer, Mitch, to get some casting advice before his upcoming session. The characters are composites, the names are fictitious and time has been compressed for this demonstration.

SFX (Ring – Ring)

MITCH: BackTrak Recording...

HAL: Mitch? This is Hal Smith from Ritem, Readim & Billum. How're you doin'?

MITCH: Great, Hal. I see we've got a session coming up tomorrow morning at nine.

HAL: Right, and I need some help finding talent.

MITCH: Kind of short notice.

HAL: Yea, I know, but the client just gave us copy approval. This should be easy though, I just need a Larry Brooks type.

MITCH: How about Larry Brooks? I hear he sounds just like himself.

HAL: I'm sure he does but I've been using him so much lately that I'd just like to use someone else.

MITCH: What is it you like about Larry? Is it his deep voice? Resonance? Strength?

HAL: Yeah, I was thinking about Ted Franklin. Doesn't he sound like that?

MITCH: He has a good strong voice but he does a radio shift til eleven, so I'm sure he couldn't make a nine A.M. session on this short notice. Do we have to do it at nine?

HAL: 'Fraid so, it has to be on the air tomorrow
night.

MITCH: Gottcha. How about Ed DeMayo?

HAL: Uhhhh, I don't know. The last time I worked
with him he was in a bad mood or somethin'.
Wouldn't take direction, complained
about the copy, and I had my client there so
it was kind of embarrassing. Is he always like
that or did I just get lucky?

MITCH: No, he's usually pretty good but I know what
you mean. He can be moody sometimes.

HAL: Well, let's keep him in mind if we can't think
of anyone else. Have you worked with Roger
Fields?

MITCH: I know a Roger Felds...

HAL: I always thought his name was Fields. Oh
well, have you worked with either of them?

MITCH: Well, I worked with Roger Felds but frankly
I wasn't impressed.

HAL: How come?

MITCH: He gets through the copy okay, but he's really
inconsistent from take to take. It makes
editing a lot harder.

HAL: We haven't got time for that.

MITCH: I wouldn't risk it. Who's the client?

HAL: It's two sixty second spots for Outerlake
Resort in southern Idaho. The copy talks
about the lush green valleys and the breath-
taking views, the usual stuff.

MITCH: So you want something warm and mellow?

HAL: Yea.

MITCH: Oh, when you said Larry Brooks I thought

you wanted strength and power. That
monster truck delivery.

HAL: No, not really. Sorry.

MITCH: No problem. That opens it up a bit. Do you
know Phil Randall?

HAL: I think he's a little too old for this.

MITCH: I'll just go down my talent list here. Mark
Michaels could probably do it.

HAL: Isn't he doing spots for Cloudburst Lodge?

MITCH: I don't know. I haven't heard any recently.

HAL: Yea, I think he is, sounds like him anyway.
I'm sure my client wouldn't go for that. How
about Richard Harper?

MITCH: He's over scale.

HAL: Is he worth it?

MITCH: Are you asking me if I think he's worth *more*
than scale?

HAL: Yea.

MITCH: No.

HAL: Fair enough, my budget can't take the hit.
You know, I used Craig Perkins a while back
and he did a great job.

MITCH: Yea, he's good, but he's got kind of a lighter
sound. He hasn't got the rich sound you want.

HAL: True, I've never heard him do much other
than that "regular guy" stuff.

MITCH: He lives out of town too, it'd be pretty short
notice to get him up here by tomorrow morning. Have you considered using a woman?

HAL: Well...

MITCH: There are some good ones.

HAL: Well...I don't know, Mitch.

MITCH: Kathy Curtis has that deeper warm voice.

HAL: Yea, but she sounds too much like a Mom to me. I'd rather have someone with more character. Isn't there a ...Marty something?

MITCH: There's Marcy Hale.

HAL: Isn't she more the character type?

MITCH: You said it, her biggest problem is sticking to the script. She's always off on some tangent. If you've got all the time in the world, she's very funny.

HAL: I can't afford the laughs. Anybody else with her character?

MITCH: Barbara Boothe is sort of her type and a very good actor.

HAL: A bit cutesy though, don't you think?

MITCH: Well, she usually starts out being cutesy but you can direct her out of it.

HAL: Do you think she can do this?

MITCH: Yea, with some direction.

HAL: Okay, we're running out of time. Let's go with her unless anyone else comes to mind.

MITCH: Ummmmm...about the only other one I can think of is Mary Masters. Her voice is a little friendlier sounding than Barbara and she's done this sort of thing before. She's new to the area but she's had lots of experience. She could probably do a nice job with this.

HAL: Really?

MITCH: Yea.

HAL: Well, I'll trust your judgment on this one. Can you book her in at nine for me?

MITCH: I'll call her agent and get back to you.

HAL: Now all I have to do is sell the idea of a
woman to the client. Does she sound
anything like Larry Brooks?

See how many ways there are for you to lose a job? And
you had no control over any of them.

Poor Larry Brooks suffered from overexposure, even
though it may have been just in the producer's mind.
Ted Franklin was never called to see about rearranging his
schedule. It was just assumed he couldn't make it.
Nobody checked with Mark to see if he really was doing a
competitor's spot. Ed, Roger and Marcy never had a
chance to redeem themselves for their past indiscretions.
Craig may have been typecast in the past, and our two
casters assumed that was all he did. Whose Mom did Kathy
sound like? Yours? Mine? The client's? Or maybe just
Hal's? Was Phil really too old, or is that just how the producer remembered him? Instead of getting over scale,
Richard got nothing, simply because he had not proven
his worth to the right person. Barbara actually had the job
until Mitch remembered one more name.

So they finally ended up with Mary, a friendly, charac-
ter-type woman who the producer had never heard
before. She's a far cry from the voice they started out to
cast. How in the world did this happen, and how do you
make sure that, if you're not the first name on the list, you
are the last?

Casting is an evaluation of four basic elements:

1. Past experience
2. Personality
3. Performance
4. Possibility

PAST EXPERIENCE takes into account everything the producers know about you. What kind of work have you done? How old are you? Have you worked with the producer before? How did it go? Are you a known commodity or a potential risk? Who's your agent? What have others said about you?

PERSONALITY relates to direct interaction. Are you easy to get along with? Are you outgoing or shy? Are you all work and no play, or all play and no work? Do you work well in a group? Do you follow direction? Can the client's wife relate to you?

PERFORMANCE is strictly your level of talent. How good are you? Can you get the job done? Is your voice right for the part? Can you read? Interpret? Can you maintain a character for sixty seconds? How versatile are you?

POSSIBILITY looks at logistics. What are the chances the producer can get you for the session? Will your schedules mesh? Can the producer afford you? Are you out of town? Are you home in bed with a sore throat? Can your agent find you in time? Do you have to drive a long way to the session?

In an ideal situation, PERFORMANCE is the only one that should really matter. But the other three points not only have an effect on casting, they are sometimes the key criteria. All this goes to show that you, as a talent, must maintain a good reputation, cultivate a pleasant demeanor and be available, in addition to being talented.

If you're a new talent you will face the PAST EXPERIENCE element head on. Producers tend to go for the safe bet. They don't like taking chances on newcomers because they can't risk failure. It's too costly and time consuming to make mistakes. Of course, you might be a great talent waiting for your big break, and producers will be quick to jump on your bandwagon — right after some other producer gives you the first call. It's an understandable reluctance. As a talent, you would probably be wary of showing up for a session where you didn't know what you'd be selling. The copywriter may have slaved away at each word in the script. The account executive may have spent long hours selling the client on the concept. The client may not be convinced that advertising works at all. The spot may be on a tight budget or a tight time frame. So, as the producer, who are you going to cast? As a newcomer on your first job, give special thanks to the producer. He or she has a lot of faith in you.

What if everyone you met had the power to hire and fire you? As a freelance actor, that's pretty much how it is. You're on display every time you're in public and your persona is being constantly assessed and analyzed. Every stage hand, recording engineer, talent agent, photographer, receptionist, writer, technician, and consumer is interested in what kind of person you are. They all can potentially affect your career. Even other talent take note of your performance and interaction. Your PERSONALITY plays a big part in whether or not you'll play a big part. You never know who might suggest your name or become your next employer down the road. News travels fast in the media business. Bad news travels even faster, so remember to keep a positive attitude and treat people with respect.

Even after the decision has been made that you have the abilities, the personality and the reputation to get the job done, the POSSIBILITY still exists that you won't get the job. You must make yourself as available as possible. You must have an answering machine, an answering service, a pager, a cellular phone or simply stay home all the time in order to know when someone wants you. The quicker you can confirm your availability the less anxious the producer and the better your chances of keeping the job. I suppose you could hang out all day in your agent's office, but you'd probably get on their nerves and they'd eventually send you out for donuts and stuff.

You also need to be flexible. Try not to make the producer or studio jump through too many hoops just to accommodate your schedule. They may be able to rearrange sessions if conflicts arise, so it never hurts to ask. However, you must remember that they could have other talent possibilities waiting to take your place. This is one profession where playing hard to get just doesn't work.

Make sure your agent is representing you fairly. He may be quoting a rate for your services that is beyond union requirements, which takes you out of the running for certain producers and projects. This is fine as long as he's working with your blessing. On the other hand, it's possible that your agent's zealous pursuit of more money may be robbing you of work and creating a bad image in the community.

If you come down sick before a session and it affects your voice or acting abilities, you owe it to your employer to report the condition as soon as possible. The decision as to whether you work or not should be made by the producer, not you. If the producer elects to continue with the session, then the producer will shoulder the responsibility for its outcome. If a decision is made to reschedule, the producer will have to take into account deadlines, studio availability and potential copy alterations. None of these can be accomplished by the talent, especially a sick one, so leave it to the producer. If the conditions make it impossible to reschedule, then recasting is necessary. You may lose the job, but you will have preserved your reputation and proven your responsibility and honesty to all concerned. They'll be back.

If you need to commute a long distance to a session, make sure you allow yourself enough time. Make sure your agent gives you fair warning, and asks the producer if you can be reimbursed for travel expenses. If travel charges are normally added to your billing, communicate this to the producer before you confirm the session. Your agent should be aware of all this and will usually take care of it for you.

Many times, the casting process for a voice acting job will begin with a taped audition. It's your one big chance to show that yours is the voice the script was truly meant for.

You see, when the writer puts an original concept on paper, there is probably a voice inside his or her head reading it back. This voice is not always their own. Many writers are very adept at creating characters and writing speech patterns quite different from the way they speak themselves.

So the writer usually has a fair idea what the spot should sound like. As a radio script makes its way through the system, however, it may undergo many changes and reinterpretations. Creative directors, account executives, the client, the client's spouse, the production company and the talent agent may all put their own particular spin on the character. So here you are walking into an audition and you need to be impressive. But to whom? Who's right? Who has the power to make the decision, and how do you know what they're thinking?

The answer is you can't know, but here are a few sug-

gestions. Check the script to see if the writer has provided
any direction for the read. Notice if the script calls for
music. If so, what kind? A notation for *ominous* and *fore-
boding* music, for instance, will tell you a lot, while a request
for *up tempo music* may only give you a hint. A notation of
appropriate music up and under won't tell you a darn thing.

Read the spot for time. Is it pretty packed with copy?
That should give you some indication of pacing.
Is the wording conversational? Is it full of long sentences
with lots of *well*s and *ya know*s? Or is it announcer
copy with short dramatic sentences and carefully crafted
words full of meaning?

If it's a TV spot you may have a written description of
the video elements. If the visuals call for *soft, misty
forest at dawn*, you should get a pretty clear picture of
your vocal style.

How about volume? If the copy contains a lot of words
such as *now, plus, call today, you won't want to miss,*
and several underlines, then you're probably looking at
hard sell. Bring up your projection level and let 'er rip.
On the other hand, if you see words such as *warm, exquisite, quiet, classic design, comfort* or *aroma,* your delivery
should reflect the appropriate mood. It's common sense
for the most part. Just look for direction words in the
copy and let them be your guide. With luck, you'll get
enough initial direction to get you through the first read.

Always give them what they ask for on the first read.
Don't try to second guess them or assume they want
you to "play" with the words or tamper with the concept.
Give it to them their way at least once.

If you get a chance to do a second read, you can let your
creative juices flow a bit more. If you really think you

can add something extra, the second take is the place to do it. Be advised, however, that you always run the risk of sounding too cocky, and the writer might object to a performance that takes too many liberties with his or her idea.

Finally, make sure your audition is of decent quality and is submitted on time. Don't make the producer wait. Then, if all goes well, you'll need to read the next chapter.

CHAPTER 9

The Recording Session

You've just thrown a bag of popcorn into the microwave when the phone rings. It's your agent. She tells you that a producer just called and said he loved your audition for Icebreaker Tire Chains. They want to book you into the studio Thursday at 10 A.M., and there will be two radio spots and one TV voice-over.

You hang up in nervous exaltation. It's your *first job! Yes!* You've arrived, it's your big break. You can feel the money in your pocket already and can imagine the demand for your talents growing and growing and...wait a minute.

What if you mispronounce the client's name? What if the producer got the talent tapes mixed up and really wants someone else? What if your car runs out of gas on the way to the session and...wait a minute.

You've been training for this moment. You know

you're talented and they "loved" your audition so what's the problem? You'll be a hot item after this, stardom is on the horizon. Today tire chains, tomorrow the…wait a minute. Is that the smell of burning popcorn?

Don't worry, the second job will be easier. To help make your sessions run smoothly, here are some observations on session procedure and hierarchy.

Before you hang up on that call from your agent, make sure you've *written down* all the important information. Don't plan on keeping it in your head. In the excitement of the moment, details can slip through so have a pencil and paper near the phone at all times. Be sure you know the correct *time* you are scheduled and *where* the session is to take place. It will help if you have compiled a list of all the possible studio addresses and phone numbers so you'll have them quickly at hand if a problem arises. Find out *who* the client is, *what* you're selling and *how much work* is involved. Is it one thirty second radio spot or a twenty-page video narration?

After you become a regular working talent, you may be faced with a few product conflicts. For instance, have you already done an ad for a competing maker of tire chains, or are you the voice of an auto parts store that sells a different brand? Your agent has some responsibility for catching conflicts but in the end you are responsible so always double check. The check should actually be done before the audition. It makes you look very bad in the producer's eyes if you audition for a job and later say you can't do it. Don't jeopardize one client for the sake of another. It's possible you may have to obtain permission from a previous client to do this job. Even if you worked for the previous client months ago, you may still be under contract.

If, for some reason, you or your agent do not catch a conflict and you somehow complete a project for a competing client, you and your agent can be held financially responsible for the re-recording/filming of the project with a conflict-free performer. In addition, you may very well lose your original client as well.

Do you have any personal conflicts? Do you object to the use of tire chains or did tire chains once cause the breakup of your marriage? Okay, so the analogy is weak, it still points out the importance of knowing who and what you're about to speak for.

You should also try to get the names of the producer and the studio engineer. These aren't critical because you will meet them at the session, but the knowledge may improve communication and efficiency once you get to the studio. It's also good to get names for your contact list and any follow-up you might wish to do.

You might ask if there is a script available ahead of time so you can better understand the character. This is particularly important in the case of long narration, or scripts with complex information or terminology. You're going to need to sound comfortable with the material so having a copy in advance could be helpful.

Find out if there's anything extra you need to bring to the session. This is common for on-camera sessions, where wardrobe and makeup may be necessary, but it's usually a foregone conclusion that the only things you need to bring to a voice-over session is your voice and your talent. A good agent will have gathered all this information for you.

On the day of the session be well-rested, even if you've been up all night worrying about it. Dress neatly and comfortably. Don't wear nylon clothing or lots of jangling

jewelry. Remember that you're going to be recorded
and this kind of stuff makes noise. Bracelets, chains and
earrings that can be easily removed are acceptable,
but plan to take them off before recording.

Here's a strange but true example of inappropriate
clothing. A talent had been called for a 9 A.M. session. She
arrived and recorded the spot without incident. When
the writer was sure he had everything he needed,
the talent was excused to go back to her regular job.

A short while later, the studio received a phone call
from the ad agency. There had been a late revision to the
script, so they needed to get the talent back into the studio
quickly. The talent was located at her job and said she
could squeeze in a session between appointments. It turns
out that she was employed by a singing telegram company
and she arrived attired in a beautiful gold harem outfit
with tiny bells attached everywhere. What little there was
of the costume was hardly removable, yet she couldn't
breathe without creating a chorus of tintinnabulation.
After several attempts, the studio engineer borrowed someone's left-behind sweatshirt from the closet and managed
to put a damper on the din long enough to get a good take.

Another true instance of unfortunate noise occurred
during an audition of new talent. The engineer set the
talent up in the booth and recorded the first take. During
the read the engineer noticed an odd clicking sound,
but attributed it to loose dentures or a noisy chair. During
take two he noticed that the clicking was rhythmic and
quite apparent. The engineer asked the talent if he had a
noisy watch or timer in the room with him.

"It's my artificial heart valve," the talent said with some
sadness, "I was afraid you might pick it up."

The engineer tried re-miking him with little success, and both finally had to agree that a career in voice-over would be difficult for him. The talent couldn't very well turn off his heart during the read, but the noise of the valve was significant enough (in the pristine environment of the studio) to be a problem. Most talent are not burdened with such problems and should only remember to dress as quietly as possible.

Plan to arrive at the studio at least ten minutes before the scheduled time. There are many reasons for this, not the least of which is that it prevents you from being late.

It's quite possible that being late is the worst offense a talent can commit. The producer, director or client can be late, but this is considered excusable since he or she is paying the bill. You may have to wait for a studio to free up, but this, too, is excusable for a short time.

When a talent holds up a session, however, tensions increase. The studio may be so tightly booked that even the slightest delay can create havoc for an entire day. The producer may be on a tight deadline or have other commitments. You don't want to walk in late to a session where the client has been adding up the minutes of unusable time.

Minutes are easily converted into dollars in this business. In 1999, depending on location, professional recording studios cost about a dollar to five dollars per minute. A producer/director may charge an equal amount. If other talent are in the spot, they could be billing around two or three dollars per minute each. Taxes, fees and equipment costs can add another buck per minute. In the event that the session involves phone patches, other studios and satellite time (more about these later), the costs can skyrocket. If you arrive 15 minutes late to the session, you may have already cost the client dearly before even opening your mouth.

Of course, there are times when you may have a perfectly good reason for being late to a session. If you know you're running late, call the studio ahead of your scheduled time and give them your estimated time of arrival. Be honest. If you know it will take you fifteen minutes, don't say ten. The client is really at your mercy because there probably isn't time to recast and call in another talent. So know how to get to the studio and consider traffic congestion at different times of the day. Make sure your transportation is reliable, as well as your watch.

For an extreme example of the importance of punctuality, consider this true story. Once one of four scheduled talent failed to show up for a session. In fact, he had so completely forgotten about it, he had gone on vacation. He had failed to notify his agent, so no one knew there was a problem until they'd been waiting in the studio for twenty minutes. Finally, a friend of the actor was contacted, and he explained where the missing actor was.

The spot had been written with this actor as the central character. There was no suitable replacement voice so the entire concept had to be scrapped for a spot hastily written and produced a day later. The client, who had incurred costs for the studio and the three other talent who had been unable to work, became so upset that he sent a bill to the missing actor. When the actor finally returned, he was shocked, saddened and very sorry. He also paid the bill. This is an extreme example, but suffice it to say that the last word on being late is DON'T.

On the positive side, being ten minutes early helps give you time to relax, get a cup of coffee, go to the bathroom, meet the other performers (who have, of course, arrived ten minutes early as well), look over the script and maybe get some initial direction from the producer.

When you arrive at the studio, check in with the front desk to make sure everyone knows you're ready.
If all is going well, they will confirm your appointment and ask you to wait until called. At the appropriate time, someone will either come and get you or you will be instructed to enter the studio on your own.

There may be many people involved in a session, or only you and the engineer. Here's a list of some of the people you might meet:

The writer
The producer
The creative director
The account executive or account supervisor
The client
The studio engineer(s)
The other talent

There are times when the producer is also the writer, creative director and account exec. I've known instances where the client is the writer and the engineer doubles as another talent.

In order to make sense of these positions, let's consider them as separate individuals who each have a unique relationship to the product and your performance.

The *writer* is usually the main director of talent. The writer has the clearest picture of the spot's concept and how it should be performed. In most cases the writer is employed by an advertising agency or is self-employed and working on a freelance basis. He or she gets credit for the concept and script, though many will insist that, in the end, clients and lawyers are the true writers. In all but some major market situations, the writer will direct the session.

The *producer* is usually also employed by the ad agency. This person has been involved in the project since the early stages. He or she has been managing the budget, coordinating schedules, booking studios, post-production facilities, talent and auditions, and keeping the project on track to meet client demands and deadlines. Producers are the ones who keep checking their watches. They also tend to spend a lot of their lives on the phone.

The *account executive* is the advertising agency's bridge to the client. This is the person who makes sure the client's desires get to the writer and the writer's ideas get back to the client. The A.E. is sort of a salesperson for the agency who tries to keep the client happy while convincing him that the agency is providing the best services possible. During a session, it may be difficult to know who the A.E. is really working for. A.E.'s may often be at odds with the creative members of their own company as they try to represent the client's sensitivities.

The *creative director* is normally the boss of the creative department at the ad agency. It is this person's job to supervise the writing staff and make sure the finished product is up to the standards set by the agency. If the creative director attends the session, he or she may take a back seat to the writer unless a problem is detected. The creative director may be more concerned with overall feeling than individual words, and may act as a conduit between A.E. and writer. You see, writers seldom believe that account people have even a smidgen of creativity while account people often see writers as devious egomaniacs more

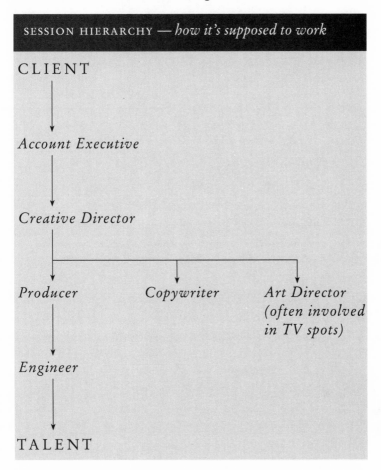

SESSION HIERARCHY — *how it's supposed to work*

CLIENT

Account Executive

Creative Director

Producer   Copywriter   Art Director
                                      *(often involved
                                      in TV spots)*

Engineer

TALENT

interested in their art than bottom-line sales.

The *client* usually doesn't attend the session. If the agency people have done their job, they will be trusted with this part of the process. The client is the ultimate bill payer (if you don't count the consumer). The client's word always prevails, and the spot isn't finished until the client says so. Clients often get a bum rap since they tend

SESSION HIERARCHY — *how it often works*

CLIENT

Account Executive ← → *Engineer*

Creative Director

Copywriter ← → TALENT

Producer

Art Director
(often involved
in TV spots)

to be conservative and safe rather than experimental and innovative in their approach to advertising. Clients can get fixated on things that have special meaning only to them, so they may give you direction that seems odd or irrelevant to the average consumer. At the same time, they can sometimes provide valuable insight or be so captivated by your performance that they delight in everything you do.

The *engineer* is the one who will set your microphone, run the equipment, keep time, slate the take numbers and keep a written log of the session. Look to the engineer for session mood, formality and pacing. How does the engineer interact with the others in the room? Is he or she treating them formally with an "all business" attitude, or is the feeling more friendly and loose? Is the engineer moving the session on at a rapid pace, or is there lots of conversation and long pauses between takes? Different directors like to work in different ways. A good engineer knows this and caters to the style of each director. By watching the engineer you should be able to tell, rather quickly, how to best deal with the entourage. The engineer may also give you direction. Sometimes it may be technical, such as how close to work the microphone, or it may be interpretive. The engineer may act as a spokesperson for a director who has difficulty verbalizing his desires.

The *other talent* got to the session the same way you did. They deserve your respect. If they have worked with this director before, you will be able to get attitude cues from them as well as the engineer. Let the director direct. Don't be too quick to tell others how to perform, and be careful of sarcastic remarks that may demean your fellow actors. The parts each actor plays may have varying degrees of difficulty. Don't trivialize the parts of others or get into an acting contest.

As I've said before, plan to do seven takes for every "director" in the room. If you're lucky, only the writer will show up.

It's no wonder some talent feel as if they're in a fishbowl while performing. This isolation is necessary, however, to keep the noises of the control room from interfering with good sound recording.

YOUR COMFORT is important to your performance and you have several options in the studio to help you feel at ease:

POSITION In most studios, you have the choice of standing or sitting during the session. You even have the option of leaning against the wall or lying down, if it will help your read. Some of this is just personal preference, but good actors will tell you that body position affects your performance as well as your comfort.

Spots that require a great deal of energy and breath control are often better delivered from a standing position. Laid-back and intimate reads may be best accomplished while sitting. If your character in the spot is doing sit-ups, then you might consider physically doing sit-ups during your performance.

The Recording Session

Studios usually supply a music stand to hold your script. This helps eliminate shuffling paper and the noise it generates. Music stands are adjustable for height. Adjust yours so your head isn't bent too far forward or back. A music stand holds two sheets of paper so you can spread out a two-page script and avoid page turning. Make sure the music stand is in an area with good lighting and that you're not reading through shadows. Often, studio lighting is controlled by dimmers that can be raised or lowered to meet your needs.

Remember that the microphone will be set to you, so take your desired position and let the engineer move the mike. Don't assume you have to stand where the mike is. It's probably left over from the last session, in a position unrelated to you.

Once you have taken your place, however, it is important not to make any large movements that might take you "off mike." Also, don't move the mike yourself after the engineer has placed it. If it's blocking your view or creating a shadow on your page, ask for assistance (more about microphones later).

If you've elected to sit and after a few takes you think you'd rather stand, just ask. The engineer can reposition the mike. Within reason, you can ask for any position you think will improve your performance. Asking for the mike to be placed on a warm sandy beach in Kauai, however, is probably outside the realm of reasonable requests.

ROOM TEMPERATURE If the room is too hot or cold, ask the engineer to adjust the thermostat. You may be spending considerable time in a small enclosed environment. If it feels uncomfortable when you walk in, it will only get worse as time passes. Speak up early and hope for the best.

HEADPHONES   Many studios will have headphones (also known as "cans") available for your use during the session. The use of headphones is an extremely emotional choice for some talent. There are those who simply cannot work without them while others insist that they are a hindrance to true acting. There is even a stigma attached to headphone use in some of the major markets. There, you are considered an announcer if you wear them and an actor if you don't. Since most voice talent today aspire to be known as actors, headphones may be kept in the closet in some big city studios.

Here are some pros and cons on the use of headphones:

Pros

Almost everyone says their recorded voice doesn't sound like them. This is because we hear ourselves from the inside where our voice resonates off our bones. The microphone tends to pick up the sound of our voice as others hear us and, like it or not, it's pretty much how we really sound. Using headphones lets us hear what the microphone is hearing. They close out the rest of the world and help us concentrate on our voice alone. They put us better in tune with the subtleties of the read and, if the volume level is increased, give us a better sense of control over our vocal "instrument." Headphones help focus our attention and let us know when we're making errors or drifting off-mike. People who don't wear headphones are afraid technology will hinder their ability to act. If that were true, then lights, microphones, and movie cameras wouldn't be part of an actor's world.

Cons

Headphones make us too aware of the technical aspects of performance such as mouth noises, diction, pitch, and presence, rather than the acting aspects of character development, expression, interaction and emotion. Headphones make us super-critical of our own work and lead to too much self-direction instead of letting the director make such decisions. Headphone wearers tend to cut themselves off in mid-read more often than non-wearers. Many times this is a great disappointment to the director. Headphones are confining and make it difficult to move and act, and are worn only by those who like to hear themselves talk.

Well, there are the arguments. It's your option. There are times when headphone use is mandatory, such as when you're reading to a pre-cut music track that must be played back during your performance, or when audio effects such as reverb or filters are added, or when you are using a phone or digital patch with a director listening in over telephone lines. Some talent say that if you're working in a group and the other talent choose to put on the "cans", then you probably should as well. The best suggestion is that you try working with and without headphones, and decide for yourself.

SOMETHING TO DRINK It's wise to have something to drink near you in the studio. Most mouth noises such as clicking and snapping are caused by a dry mouth. Talent use a variety of concoctions to keep their mouths and throats in shape. Herb tea, a honey and lemon mixture,

cough drops, ice water, throat spray, strong coffee
and sour candies have all been used to improve and enrich
vocal tones. Basically, warm liquids such as coffee, tea
or even warm water do a good job of keeping the mouth
damp and the throat clear. Singers have long known to stay
away from milk or chocolate before a performance,
and the same holds true for commercial voice talent. If you
normally suffer from a dry mouth, you might purchase
a bottle of saliva substitute. It's a wetting agent that can be
sprayed directly into the mouth. It's available in drug
stores without a prescription.

Since good diction and clear thinking are important in
the studio, alcoholic beverages are a big no-no.

WRITING INSTRUMENT You should always have a pen or
pencil with you in the studio. You can bring one from
home if you like, or borrow one. The studio is likely to
already have pencils in the booth for your convenience.
Some talent like to use colored highlight pens to mark
their script.

PLAYBACK You have the right to ask for a playback of your
performance at any time during the session. Playbacks
are important because they give you a chance to really listen
to yourself. Many talent find a playback quite helpful in
detecting shifts in character and vocal weaknesses. Ask
the engineer for a playback whenever you feel the need,
but keep in mind that playbacks require time. Ask for
them judiciously so you don't slow the session too often.

YOUR OPINION You are not being hired for your voice
alone. The session demands that you use all those things

that make you a talented actor. If you have an opinion on such things as presentation, characterization, timing or even copy changes, your views will probably be welcome. It is customary and respectful to read the copy as written and as directed at least a few times before offering any suggestions of your own. Remember the session hierarchy. By all rights, you should have to listen to everyone else's opinion first, but usually you'll have the opportunity to make a few comments as the session rolls on.

One line often repeated by some talent is, "If you're happy, I'm happy." Frankly, this can indicate a lack of real concern on the part of the talent. It's as if they're using the client's ears and not their own. Good actors, it seems, can feel a good performance inside themselves, regardless of whether they hear any applause. If you want other people to care about your work, you'll need to start with some care of your own.

These are about all the options you have, but they should allow you to get comfortable and into the proper mood for the perfect performance.

You'll have to bring some of that proper mood with you as well. Some talent make the awful mistake of entering the studio with woeful tales of their horrible morning, car troubles, cat at the vet and all number of other calamities that help get the session off to a dismal start. No director wants to know you're in a bad mood when you start to read his copy. If you have to let loose, do it after the session or, better yet, in your car before you come in. Your state of mind should be up and positive. If it isn't, you should call on some of your acting ability to convince everyone that you couldn't be happier.

All this brings us, finally, to the recording process itself.

The session is done in "takes". A take may be a reading of the full script, or just a portion of the script. Usually the engineer "slates" them ("Take one", "take two", etc.) in numerical order. The slate is recorded at the start of each take and provides an audible identification to help locate parts later during the editing phase.

A written log is also kept by the engineer. On it, he or she notes the take numbers, the timing of each take, what the take consisted of and any relevant comments about the performance.

Unless instructed otherwise, you should start each take from the top, that is, the beginning, of the copy. Starting part way through the copy is called a "pick-up."

If the director wants you to do a pick-up at a certain line, it's customary to start one line sooner and read into the pick-up. This "read-in" helps get your projection level, tone and breaths in the proper place so the pick-up take and the master take will match. You should assume that a pick-up goes to the end of your script.

A pick-up that requires you to do only a certain segment in the middle of the copy is called an "insert". You should read in to an insert as well. Sometimes you may be asked to do an insert on a single line. Usually on a short segment like this, the engineer will ask for an "ABC." This means you should read it three times on the same slate number. You can do a read-in if you like but it's not necessary. Just take a comfortable pause between each read. Normally, the director is listening for different deliveries, so don't make all three readings the same.

Most of the time, the finished spot is made up of many pieces pulled from several takes. Some talent view this as a personal failure since they couldn't give the director a perfect read from start to finish. The reality is, however, that getting every nuance and every necessary inflection into one read is extremely difficult. It is considered easier to assemble the perfect read by editing the best parts of several takes together than to spend time waiting for it to happen. Some talent brag about being "One Take Wonders." Don't bet on it. Directors who accept the first take are either naive or undiscriminating. A director isn't doing the job if he or she doesn't direct. In the final analysis, the first take may indeed end up being the best take, but without doing others for comparison, who's to know? As far as you're concerned, try to make take one the perfect take, but plan on doing twenty more.

If you make a mistake or lose your place during a take, you should always try to keep going unless the director or engineer interrupts. Don't self-direct unless you become so completely lost that you simply can't go on. An incomplete take, sometimes called a "false start", may still be usable. By editing a false start to a pick-up, a full read can be obtained. Nothing is thrown away. Sometimes even rehearsal takes and practice reads are recorded. It's not uncommon to edit single words, or even parts of words, out of one take and into another. Voice talent should not be overly concerned about doing too many takes. It's a normal condition and you should realize that multiple takes are not always a sign of poor performance. The fact is, if you were really *that* bad, you would probably be excused from the session long before you had a chance to do all those takes.

Most sessions are friendly and cooperative events. Everyone is there to get the best possible product and each individual brings his or her unique talents. There are, on rare occasions, a few tension-filled sessions where the incentive will be to get it done quickly rather than get it done right. You'll be able to tell when you've entered this type of session. It's the kind of voice job when your best ally may be knowing when to keep your mouth shut.

CHAPTER 10

The Script

THE BROTHER of a well-respected voice talent once jokingly said, "It's a bit embarrassing having a relative who makes *spots* for a living." The industry term "spot" has been used frequently in this book and actually originated during the early days of broadcasting. It comes from the phrase "on the spot" which was used to describe all material that ran between scheduled programs, and was usually produced live. Today, all forms of short-format broadcast advertising, whether produced live or not, are still called spots.

Advertising is simply an organization of words and ideas designed to convince the recipient to alter, or to reinforce, his action, behavior or opinion.

There's a great definition someone concocted to explain advertising:

"Advertising is the science of arresting human intelligence long enough to get money from it."

Let's face it, we've all been molded and shaped by advertising. It's the reason we believe one detergent is better than another. It's the reason we care which shoe a star athlete wears or which charity deserves our contribution. Advertisers pour billions of dollars into enticing, cajoling, provoking, beckoning, browbeating, convincing, inspiring, duping, serenading, hounding, appealing, pressuring, motivating, seducing and embarrassing us into buying their product or service. They place much of their faith in communicating their ideas through the use of words.

Whether it's print, television or radio, all advertising starts with words. For broadcast spots, these words present the concept and eventually take the form of a script. Scripts come in many shapes and styles and several samples will be presented in this chapter. (By the way, those of you who wish to work on losing your sibilance problems may wish to use that last sentence for practice.)

You'll usually get the script only a few minutes before performing it. Some scripts are written in haste, but for the most part, they are examples of hard work. Artistic agonies of the creative writer aside, the script has probably been rewritten and "polished" by everyone from the creative director to the client's sister's husband (he used to be a writer, you know), and everyone in between.

Then the least creative of all entities enters the picture — the *Legal Department*. These people make sure that all claims are provable, all endorsements are authorized, and all statements are clear. Consequently, a lot of the creative art that may have originally existed may be lost. It's the reason many ads talk for sixty seconds and never really say anything. The resulting copy, which may have started as a cohesive arrangement of words, is now strewn with disclaimers, qualifiers, vehicle identification numbers, meaningless adjectives and five extra mentions of the client's name.

Make no mistake, the input of others and the legality of the finished product are not items to be taken lightly. This chain of command is an important aspect of the system, and as a voice talent, you need to know that the spot you have been handed is often a product of considerable effort. Treat it with some degree of respect. No matter what its condition when it arrives, it's pretty amazing that it's gotten to you at all.

Your director will probably give you some initial direction, but there's plenty of direction to be found in the script as well. A quick glance can answer several questions, such as: How fast will you need to read it? Where are the emphasis words? Where can you take breathing pauses? What mood is called for? Are there any "direction" words in the copy?

As you look at your first script, one other question you should ask is, "Can I *see* it?" It's surprising how many talents routinely neglect to wear glasses or other corrective eyewear that will help them see clearly. It may be vanity, image consciousness or forgetfulness, but it's an unnecessary hassle for everyone involved in the session. If you need glasses, wear them! Don't worry that they may "ruin" your appearance. Nobody looks at you during an audio session anyway.

Let's look over a sample radio script and address all these questions individually. Don't bother reading for interpretation yet.

Hamilton Motors
HM R3095-23
'Your Good Name'
:30 Radio

ANNC:

Today at Hamilton Motors, we have a car with your name on it. That's right, if your name is Packard, DeSoto, Nash, Hudson, Kaiser, Tucker or Edsel, we have a classic collector car waiting for you. Even if you don't share a moniker with one of these beautifully restored vehicles, your good name still gets quality service, friendly advice and genuine respect at Hamilton Motors. So come in and visit with a few illustrious names of the past. And add your own to a growing family of Hamilton Motors customers. Hamilton Motors. Where you can put a classic of the past in your future.

The Script

What did you learn from your initial scan? Some of the obvious points are that the client is a car dealer, that you have thirty seconds to read it, and that it's written for an announcer in first-person present tense. Now let's look a little closer. The spot code number at the top of the page is something you'll need for your billing and records. There are many types of coding but this is fairly common. The prefix "HM" is a shortened version of the client's name. The "R" stands for "radio", the "30" for the spot length and the "95" for the year it was written. The "23" means that this is the twenty-third spot written for the client during the year. If the last two numbers are high in a spot code like this, it means this client is a heavy user of advertising. This is a good thing when you're looking for those profitable on-going accounts. You're likely to see many variations of this spot coding format. Most talent pass over it with little consideration, but it can be a source of information that you may find helpful.

Did you run across any words that were unclear? How about pronunciation? Are you familiar with all the car names? The spot starts with a joke (a small one) so you can assume that your approach should be friendly with a touch of smile. Now look for "direction" words. These are usually adjectives that refer to the product, but are also words with an attitude or style. In this script we find the words "classic", "beautifully", "quality", "friendly", "genuine" and "illustrious". These words come with built-in interpretation and you should use them to guide your own interpretation of the script. The title of the spot is "Your Good Name". This, too, has an attitude. The writer has distilled the essence of the spot into this three-word title so if you see it again in the copy, you may wish to give it a little extra vocal oomph. All this script analysis takes only seconds to perform. As your experience increases, it will become automatic.

Next, you'll need to start reading the script aloud. This will help show you places for emphasis and breathing. What words should get more emphasis? Start with the client's name, for one. No talent ever lost a job because they made too much of the client's name. We already mentioned that the phrase "your good name" should get something extra. Perhaps parts of the phrase should as well. Look for any reference to "your", "good" and "name" to see if they can use some help. Also look for contrasting words. A good example in this script is in the last line, where you need to contrast "past" and "future." A call to action also gets emphasis. A call to action is simply a word or phrase that asks or demands that the listener do something. Here we find two examples: "So come in…" and "add your own." That gives you plenty of emphasis points, and the director hasn't even started to add hers.

Emphasis can be accomplished in a variety of ways. Increased volume can do the trick. So can over-enunciation. Good voice actors also give emphasis by reading the word slower, by setting it off with a slight pause before and after and by varying pitch. Read the phrase "we have a car with your name on it" aloud, giving every word equal emphasis. Now read it again and raise your eyebrows when you come to the word "your." As you do this, let your voice follow your eyebrows. Don't just read it louder. Let the listener hear your eyebrow movement come through your voice.

Now try it a different way. This time we need a bigger

physical move. As you come to the word "your," point your finger at the imaginary listener. Use your whole arm and give it that Uncle Sam approach. Once again, we don't really want an increase in volume, we just want an increase in emphasis. We want to hear you pointing. Did it feel different? Did it sound different? It should. You constantly use emphasis in your everyday speech. It's no different here, except that you're speaking someone else's words. That ability is what separates the actor from the rest of the world. By using varying degrees of eyebrow raising and pointing you can get through this script just fine. Run through the whole spot once and try to cover all the direction we've talked about.

You probably noticed that it's pretty hard to keep all that direction in your head. What you really need is some way of writing it on the page without messing up the copy. That's the next step, and we'll use a new script to give you some hints.

KBS9030-02
KURTZ Brand Sausage
"Oktoberfest Favorite"
Beaumont

(uptempo oompah music up and under)

VOX: KURTZ, THE OFFICIAL SAUSAGE OF OKTOBERFEST, IS NOW AVAILABLE IN YOUR FAVORITE SUPERMARKET. THE SWEET SMOKEY FLAVOR AND WONDERFUL AROMA OF KURTZ BRAND GERMAN SAUSAGE WILL DELIGHT EVERY MEMBER OF YOUR FAMILY. KURTZ SAUSAGE IS MADE FROM 100 PERCENT PURE BEEF AND A SECRET BLEND OF SPICES FOR A GREAT TASTE. AT PICNICS, TAILGATE PARTIES, BACKYARD BARBECUES, BREAKFAST, LUNCH OR DINNER, CELEBRATE OKTOBERFEST ALL YEAR LONG WITH THE 'OFFICIAL FAVORITE' -- KURTZ BRAND GERMAN SAUSAGE.

(live annc. tag)
PICK UP KURTZ SAUSAGE AT SYDNEY'S FINE FOODS IN WESTRIDGE.

The Script

You probably noticed some differences between this script and the last one. For one thing, the spot code number is in a slightly different form. In this case the "KBS" stands for "Kurtz Brand Sausage", "90" is the year, "30" is the spot length and "2" means it's the second spot of the year. It's not important that you understand all spot codes but they do make an interesting puzzle sometimes. "Beaumont", in the header, is probably the writer's name.

An extra direction clue has been given to you right off the top. The spot calls for music. Not just any music, but *up-tempo oompah music*. Right away, you know you're going to have to compete with a boisterous backing track. That probably means you'll need to raise your projection and keep your enthusiasm high. You may be able to get a playback of the music as you read, or it may be added later. You'll still have to hear the music in your head regardless of whether it's real or imagined.

The abbreviation "vox" is a common substitution for "voice." In other words, it means you. Another abbreviation you'll run across is "vo" for "voice-over." At the bottom of the page you see something called "Live Annc Tag." This part of the spot is to be added later at the radio station by a different announcer. There will probably be various versions of this tag, each one mentioning a different location. The live tag affects your read in one important way. You must allow enough time for the tag to be added and still be finished in thirty seconds. In this case, you have about twenty seven seconds for your part and three seconds for the tag.

Look over the spot again and try to find other direction hiding in the copy. Follow the same analysis we talked about on the last spot. The direction words are a little harder to find in this spot, but there are a few. "Now" implies urgency so it tends to underscore the up-tempo attitude we get from the music. "Celebrate" says excitement and flamboyance. "Wonderful" means…well…you know…just be full of wonder. With that concise direction in mind, go back and read the spot aloud. If you have a stopwatch, run a time on yourself.

Okay, now the director has decided to cut copy. You're having to read too fast to squeeze it all into your allotted time. He also wants you to hit a few words harder, put a little more "music" in your voice, and add a bit more "energy." After a few more takes, you've altered your script to look something like this:

KBS9030-02
KURTZ Brand Sausage
"Oktoberfest Favorite"
Beaumont

(uptempo oompah music up and under)

<u>VOX:</u> KURTZ, THE OFFICIAL SAUSAGE OF ~~THIS~~ this year's

OKTOBERFEST, IS NOW AVAILABLE IN YOUR

FAVORITE SUPERMARKET. THE SWEET|SMOKEY

FLAVOR||AND WONDERFUL AROMA OF KURTZ

BRAND GERMAN SAUSAGE WILL DELIGHT ~~EVERY~~

~~MEMBER OF~~ YOUR FAMILY. KURTZ SAUSAGE IS

MADE FROM 100 PERCENT PURE BEEF|AND|A

SECRET BLEND OF SPICES FOR ~~A GREAT~~ an unforgettable TASTE.

AT PICNICS, TAILGATE PARTIES, BACKYARD

BARBECUES, ~~BREAKFAST LUNCH OR DINNER,~~ or anytime

CELEBRATE OKTOBERFEST ALL YEAR LONG WITH

THE 'OFFICIAL FAVORITE'|-| KURTZ BRAND

GERMAN SAUSAGE.

(live annc. tag)
PICK UP KURTZ SAUSAGE AT SYDNEY'S FINE
FOODS IN WESTRIDGE.

One of the great accomplishments of the professional voice talent is the ability to read through this kind of jumble and act at the same time. Can you decipher the code, figure out what the director wanted and deliver the perfect read? Here are some hints. The up and down arrows are indications of vocal inflection. If we use the same analogy as before, you can think of them as up and down eyebrows. The vertical straight lines are pauses, a single line for a short pause and a double line for a longer pause. There are a couple of added words and the crossed-out words have been deleted to give you more time. There are many more script marking devices. A voice-over or acting class will teach you several more techniques. You can make up your own as well. The idea is simply to give yourself some visual clues without making the script unreadable. Try reading the edited script a couple times using the visual direction. Then move on to the next script.

The Script

NORTH HARBOR PEST CONTROL
:30 TV
"Safe"

VIDEO   AUDIO

BLACK   MUSIC: Low drone
Fade up on white type   ANNC: In 1944, the
saying "1944"   suggested treatment against
                                     termites and carpenter
Fade to BLACK   ants was the use of:
Cut to THIOCYANATE   Thiocyanate,
Cut to CALCIUM CYANIDE   Calcium Cyanide,
Cut to LEAD ARSENATE   Lead Arsenate,
Cut to KEROSENE   and Kerosene.
Fade to BLACK   The insects weren't the
                                     only ones in danger.

                                     (MUSIC BRIGHTENS)
Fade up on "1998" type   Today, North Harbor Pest
                                     Control uses only safe,
Fade to action footage   odorless products approved
of North Harbor   by the Environmental
experts performing jobs.   Protection Agency.
                                     North Harbor treatments
                                     are safe for you, your
                                     children and your pets.

Fade to logo & phone #
                                     Call North Harbor
                                     Pest Control.
                                     Eliminate your problems.
                                     Keep your peace of mind.

This script is for a TV spot. As you can see, there's something going on visually as well as audibly. Even though you're the voice talent, you need to be aware of what's happening on screen as you're speaking. Just because it says video on the header doesn't mean it's none of your business. Quite the opposite. The video description can clue you in to direction just as your own words can. Look for images and attitudes. Look for colors and visual effects. Look for design elements and point of view.

In this particular case, many of the images are just white lettering on a black background. The words fill the screen. It's as if they are being photographed extremely close-up for dramatic impact. A close-up is often indicated by the abbreviation "CU" in the visual description.

You can vocally handle a close-up in two ways. If it is a close-up of something large and dramatic, such as the jaws of a great white shark, you can play it big and loud and powerful. If, on the other hand, the image is something small, you should pull your volume back, soften your approach and talk as if you're looking through a microscope rather than sitting in a movie theater.

Which style do you think is appropriate for this spot? At what speed should you read it? What kind of attitude do you think the spot has? How will that affect your read? For contrast, try reading it with a strong, no-nonsense approach and then try a soft, intimate read. Which do you like best?

One other point to note in this spot is that the words "pets" and the word "pests" are read very close together. They look fine in print but could be a problem when spoken. Be careful with your diction.

Before we move on to the next script, let's take a second

and talk about time. In fact, let's take about thirty seconds and sixty seconds. These two times will become integral to your life as a voice talent. They are the standard length of television and radio ads. There are other possibilities, such as ten second, fifteen second and ninety second spots, but the vast majority fall into the minute and half minute formats.

Radio has a small amount of "slop time" due to its looser and more manually-driven style. Precise timing is not always critical. A radio spot might run for sixty-one seconds or fifty-eight and a half seconds without causing problems. Radio stations will tell you, however, that accurate timing is preferred.

The computer-driven world of TV has no latitude at all. The computers that play the commercials are precisely timed and require a half second to get one spot off and the next one on. Therefore, a thirty second TV spot must be completed in twenty-nine and a half seconds to allow for this exact cueing. Even the slightest extension of this time will be cut off at air time.

For the most part, scripts tend to be overwritten. No matter how much time is available, writers usually fill it up, and when you think about it, it's quite understandable. They have a difficult job trying to squeeze into a minute or less all the copy points, character development, story line, prices, addresses, phone numbers, punch lines, slogan lines, and possibly a small part for the client's seven year old son. If the copywriter has a hard time accomplishing this task, your job may be difficult as well. The ticking clock can be an irritant to everyone involved in the project. The writer may have to limit his concept or number of characters, the talent may have to emote less than she'd like, the audio engineer may have to cut production elements shorter than normal. The entire project may be under a tight deadline that doesn't allow experimentation or group participation. However, time can also be the catalyst that leads to more creativity. It can help keep the spot from becoming complex or wordy. A tight deadline for completion can prevent drawn-out decision making and production by committee.

The best voice talents have internal clocks. When the director asks them to pick up three seconds in their read, they know how much faster they have to go to get it. Experiment with time. Get a stopwatch and practice keeping time in your head. Time yourself reading a magazine ad and try to guess how long it took before looking at the watch.

Instead of exact time, a director may ask you to "take a beat" between lines. If you think of this in musical terms, a beat is one count of whatever tempo you've set from the start. A beat can also be described as a moment of thought. If you've been reading fast, your character's thought time is probably short. If you've been delivering the copy at a leisurely pace, your thought time may be somewhat longer. Therefore, "a beat" is an imprecise form of measurement whose length is set more by feel than by a stopwatch.

You'll need help with the next script. It's a dialogue piece, so find a friend.

CINEMAGIC
"Never Heard of It"
:60 Radio

vox 1   I'm here to tell you all about Springfield's new CineMagic Theater...

vox 2   Never heard of it.

vox 1   With classic movies and featuring real buttered popcorn...

vox 2   I don't know that film, who's in it?

vox 1   Plus a jukebox in the lobby...

vox 2   That one I know! It starred James Dean, right?

vox 1   [*finally acknowledging* vox 2] Look, I'm talking about a real CD jukebox filled with classic film scores so you can pick the theater music that plays before the movie and during intermission.

vox 2   Ingrid Bergman and Leslie Howard, 1935!

vox 1   What are you talking about?

vox 2   Intermission!

vox 1   [*frustrated*] Ohhh! CineMagic also features 70mm projection on a screen specially designed for 70mm, the brightest picture in town, rocking seats with lots of leg room and an incomparable sound system that puts you right into the movie.

vox 2   Neat trick.

vox 1   That's why they call it CineMagic.

annc   Tonight CineMagic presents *The Sound of Music*. CineMagic, where the theater is part of the show.

VOX 2 You know, they should build a theater like that.
VOX 1 *They did*! It's on SE 31st & Claremont,
        and you are a *wacko*.
VOX 2 Didn't Hitchcock direct that?
VOX 1 [*sigh*]

Which part did you chose to do? This spot takes a traditional form of dialogue commercials. You have the know-it-all voice of reason for the message, and the uninformed antagonist for comic relief. Spots such as this require expert timing on the part of both actors. Rapid fire delivery helps make the spot humorous. The performers will have to be tight to the end of each other's lines.

It is extremely important to treat your co-performer with respect. A session is not a contest. Your objective is to work together to get the best possible product. The two talent who are thrown together for this brief exercise in teamwork may not have equal abilities. If your partner is having difficulty, you may make suggestions to improve the situation. Try not to criticize. If you are paired with a more experienced actor, don't be afraid to ask for help. He or she may be able to suggest alternate approaches or may be able to give you a better "set-up" through his or her own performance. You will never show weakness by trying to improve your performance. When it comes to dialogue spots, the final product will sound its best when everyone contributes their best.

There is no better training for commercial voice-over than practice. Reading scripts, ads, books, articles, jokes, menus, catalogues, billboards or even fortune cookies aloud will help make you a better talent. Whether you do it in a class or by yourself, interpreting the written word is the basis for this craft.

However, too much practice can be detrimental. Unlike the stage actor, who must memorize his part, commercial voice actors are usually at their best when they are spontaneous and unrehearsed. Many copywriters and directors are reluctant to give talent a script in advance for fear the talent will memorize the lines. Once he has memorized the script, it is often difficult to direct a talent to change pacing, pauses, or inflection. If a copywriter wants to rearrange the words or cut copy, the talent will have to overcome the original memorized script. In some cases, over-practice makes imperfect. Don't memorize copy. Look through it for direction hints and possible problems, but after that, wait for your director.

On the following pages, a variety of writers have submitted scripts for you to try. You'll see the various ways scripts are presented. Use the techniques we've discussed to look for direction words, attitude, pacing, and projection.

The copywriter is the architect of the ad. The talent is the carpenter. The script is the blueprint. The studio engineer provides all the necessary construction materials.

As the talent, you choose your tools and use them wisely, adding your own expertise and craftsmanship to build the copywriter's dream into a thing of beauty. And then, when it's all over, your brother comes in and says he's embarrassed because you make *spots* for a living! Oh, well.

My thanks to copywriters Stephany Hale, Jamie Barrett, Johnny Gunn, Teresa Elliot, Jamie Leopold, Jackie Hallock, Dave Newman and Joan Vallejo for allowing me to reprint these scripts.

In script one for KPTV, your part is typed in caps.
The lower case lines are taken from the soundtrack of the
movie being advertised and are called "sound bites."
You will be actually interacting with dialogue from the
film. Have some fun with this one and keep your energy
level high.

Script two is for Nike Town in Portland, Oregon. The
copy calls for a "guy" but there's no reason a woman
can't read it as well. Try taking a low-key or flat approach.
There are plenty of direction words to help get you into
character.

Script three for Lander Looms is self-explanatory.

The fourth script for The Water Tower requires good
breath control and lots of quick attitude shifts. Men
can read this by changing a couple words. Remember to
keep your character nice. It is Christmas, after all.

For the fifth script, you may wish to listen to a little of
the West Side Story soundtrack for some musical attitude.
You're even given a chance to sing a little if you like.

Script six sets out to sell a city to potential visitors
with a good private-eye character. Women can read this
one as well.

Script seven for the Orange County Nike Town
features a bitter old man. A bitter old woman might like
to try it, too.

We return to KPTV for script eight. This time your
attitude needs to change from wild and crazy to tense and
dramatic.

Script nine is for Maxey Toyota. It's all about surprises
so your performance should reflect it. It's also written in
first-person conversational style so don't forget to make
it personal. This is what we call "one-on-one" copy —

just pretend you're talking directly to one person, such as a relative or good friend.

The tenth piece of copy for the Oregon Dairy Commission is an example of an editing script. The circled numbers are selected takes that the director wants the engineer to pull out of the raw recorded material for each section. The director will then review these takes and will narrow the selections even more until the best take is found. This script isn't meant for you to read. It's here to give you some idea of how spots can be assembled from many different reads. It also shows how the script itself is edited and re-worked.

VOICE-OVERS

735 S.W. 20th Place

P.O. Box 3401

Portland, Oregon 97208

Phone (503) 222-9921

A Chris-Craft Station   Oregon Television, Inc.

KPTV [12]

:60 Radio Script "The Good, The Bad and
The Ugly / Every Which Way But Loose"

Copywriter: Stephany L. Hale
Promotion Producer

TONIGHT ON KPTV 12....   :02
    SFX Gunshots   :02
THE GOOD....   :01
    "Every gun makes it's own tune."   :02
THE BAD....   :01
    "That's why they pay me."   :01
AND THE UGLY....   :01
    "I get dressed. I kill them. Be right back."   :02
CLINT EASTWOOD...LEE VAN CLEEF...AND ELI WALLACH..."THE GOOD, THE BAD AND THE
UGLY"....   :05½
    "Nice family."   :01
TONIGHT AT 8.   :01

        (19½)   (:08)   (:11½)

AND TOMORROW NIGHT ON TV 12....   :02
    "God, you're a handsome devil."   :01½
CLINT'S BACK, IN ABOUT THE FUNNIEST FLICK YOU COULD EVER BUST A GUT OVER!   :04
    "What is it?"   :01
IT'S FIST FIGHTS...AND MONKEY BUSINESS, AND FIST FIGHTS...AND BUXOM BLONDES, AND
FIST FIGHTS...AND "BAD" BIKERS AND FIST FIGHTS...AND MEAN OLD LADIES...AND FIST
FIGHTS, WELL...YOU'LL GET THE PICTURE! IT'S THAT KNOCKOUT COMEDY EVERYONE JUST
GOES APE OVER, "EVERY WHICH WAY BUT LOOSE"!

SO, CATCH CLINT, TONIGHT AT 8 IN, "THE GOOD, THE BAD AND THE UGLY, AND TOMORROW
NIGHT AT 7:30 IN, "EVERY WHICH WAY BUT LOOSE" – BOTH, ON KPTV 12.   :26
    "You're full of all kinds of surprises, these days."   :03

        (:37½)   (:05½)   (:32)

        (:57)   (:13½)   (:44)

SCRIPT ONE

The Script

WIEDEN & KENNEDY

COPY

CLIENT: Nike
TITLE: Nike Town Portland Radio "Street Names" :55
JOB #:   NST NTN 03692
VERSION: 2
DATE: 2/26/92

COPY:
GUY: Wanna keep California-types from moving to Portland? Simple. Change the street names. Lovejoy, for example. It's too warm, too welcoming. And Yamhill. Conjures up images of sweet potatoes rolling down gently sloping streets. That kind of thing only happens in nice, liveable cities. Then there are those shiny, fuzzy-sounding names like Sunnyside Road. Sunnyview Court. Sun Meadow Lane. Why no street names that capture true Portland living? Like "Torrential Downpour" Drive? "Monsoon" Lane? Or "We Have No Pro Football Team And We're Very Bitter About It" Road. The second problem is Nike Town. Nike Town puts Portland over the top. Who wouldn't pick up stakes and head for Rose City once they discover they can shop among amazing life-like statues of Michael Jordan and Bo Jackson? And what smart shopper wouldn't rent a U-Haul the instant they learn Nike Town stocks the newest and widest selection of merchandise and displays it in an innovative and ever-changing retail environment? You're sending out the wrong message, Portland. Stop looking so contented all the time. Wipe the grin off your face. Let the shoulders sag a bit. Learn to sulk. Trust me, you'll be much happier.

PRODUCT/MOUSE:
1-800#:

RADIO COPY

**LANDER LOOMS.
"OVERACTOR"
:60 RADIO SPOT**

ANNC: And now, an over-actor speaks on behalf of Lander Looms.

DELIVERY SHOULD BE IN A VERY OVERLY DRAMATIC FASHION AS IF EACH WORD WAS AS GOLDEN AS THE ACTOR'S OWN SELF IMAGE.

ACTOR: It was more, much more than an oriental rug. It was a work of exquisite art, a magnificent meadow woven beneath me. Yet mere words do not adequately measure the splendor of pattern, texture, color and design. Like some sumptuous slipper enfolding my feet in wondrous wool. Lander Looms had brought me more than a rug, they had brought me pleasure, style, grace and (starts to fade out) a new outlook on life. Life -- what is life? It is a harmonious blending -- a weaving, if you will, that

ANNC: Lander Looms. Sometimes, just talking about our oriental rugs can be pretty exciting.

ACTOR: Lander Looms had left me absolutely speechless. (pause) I mean the charismatic colors consumed my vision (begin fade out).....and catapulted my senses toward Utopian...

SCRIPT THREE

The Script

ADVERTISING & DESIGN

RADIO COPY

Client: The Water Tower
Project: Christmas radio spot

Announcer: woman, early to mid forties
Sound effects throughout and music

Anncr:

It's night and I'm standing on the edge of a tall building...across the city, hundreds of
Christmas lites blink on and off... I spread my arms and do a perfect swan dive ... I'm
flying over the city - what am I after?... Christmas shopping! I fly towards a huge mall
crammed with thousands of wild eyed shoppers, pushing and shoving ...ripping things off
the shelves and crowding into long lines - this is a nightmare , so I shoot back up into the
night sky, ..now I'm being drawn towards a large round tower (sfx - kerplunk) suddenly
I'm inside, I'm under water... but it's o.k... I'm completely relaxed and there are dozens of
wonderful shops all with the most unique and interesting gifts I've ever seen...with
friendly people who wave and smile as I float by....suddenly a miniature Santa Claus
appears
" Merry Christmas" he says... I'm about to reply when my eyes pop open, it's my husband
shaking me... "honey wake up," he says, "we need to get an early start on our Christmas
shopping." I break out in a cold sweat. "Don't worry," he says, "we'll skip the malls and
go to the Water Tower. It's much more comfortable, and they've got great shops and
restaurants—we can do all of our shopping and find something special for everyone on
our list and ...Hmm I think, The Water Tower at John's Landing.... shopping under
water... that seems somehow familiar... but I can't exactly remember why ...

VOICE-OVERS

AUGUST PLEDGE '92
WEST SIDE STORY

:60 RADIO

AUDIO	VOICE OVER
(Music - Sharks/Jets intro)	Listen, I need your help, there's this great little movie coming on Oregon Public Broadcasting tonight at 8. No, that's not the problem. The problem is how to let everyone know about it?
	Oh! the name? It's called West Side Story. You know? The Sharks. The Jets. Tony. Maria. Natalie Wood, Rita Marino, Music by Leonard Bernstein? No bells huh? How about Tonight, tonight.
(music - Tonight)	Yeah! like that.
	Sure it's a musical, but it's a classic.
	It has romance.
"Maria, I love you..." It's dangerous if Bernardo Knew..."	
"We're gonna clean those sharks up..."	It has Action.
	and great dancing.
	West Side Story. Some people think of it as Romeo and Juliet in New York. We like to think of it as, a great movie.
(music - America)	That's West Side Story tonight at 8 on OPB TV. It's where you belong.

The Script

COPY

Client: Lincoln City
Media: Radio
Size: :60
Date: 2/91

THE DETECTIVE

SFX: "Mike Hammeresque" music

ANNCR: I'd accepted the job for the ususal reason. I needed the
          money. Finding her wouldn't be easy, but her photo told
          me I had to try. The last thing she said before she
          disappeared was that she had to get away. Not much of a
          clue. Friends said she loved the Oregon coast -- especially
          Lincoln City. It was worth a shot. If I didn't find her at
          least I could play a few holes of golf. Hike up to Cascade
          Head. Check out the antique stores and boutiques and
          the national brand factory outlet stores. What had I
          heard? "Lincoln City. Where shopping really is a day at
          the beach." Women love to shop, right? I'd have to
          check out all the tucked-away restaurants, but first I
          decided to check the hotels. They have more than 2,000
          rooms with ocean views; maybe she'd decided to curl up
          with a good look. Then again, maybe she was out there.
          Somewhere. Flying a kite. You know what they say
          about Lincoln City. The beach is just the beginning.

VO: Call 1-800-452-2151. Lincoln City. We'll help you find
          yourself.

ANNCR: (In background) I saw footprints in the sand. Maybe they
          weren't hers, maybe they were. I took off my shoes. I
          had to find out.

ADVERTISING AND PUBLIC RELATIONS   2445 NW IRVING STREET   PORTLAND, OREGON 97210   503/224-1711   FAX 503/224-3026

SCRIPT SIX

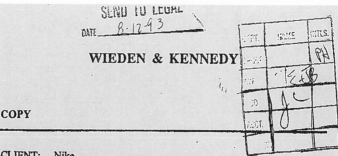

SEND TO LEGAL

DATE 8-12-93

WIEDEN & KENNEDY

COPY

CLIENT: Nike
TITLE: Orange County Radio - Sports
JOB #:   NST ORAR 14594
VERSION: 1
DATE: 8/12/93
TEAM: Jamie & Teresa

COPY:

ANNCR: And now, a bitter old man for Nike Town.

ED: I tell ya, you can't turn on the TV these days without seeing some punk kid tryin some newfangled sport. You call jumpin off a bridge with a rubber band around your foot sports?! In my day we played a game called football, in a cow pasture with a rotting cow pie for a ball! Cow pie in the face, now that's sport! You wanna talk basketball?! I'll tell you basketball - a rotting gunny sack nailed to a dead tree and *more* cow pies! And you punks think you know about locker rooms? Back then, we changed in a rotting outhouse, ten, twelve of us at a time! And liked it! Uniforms? Rotting animal skins! Cause we were tough! Today you punk kids got your Nike Town, with all those air cushioned clothes and newfangled spandex shoes. You don't know shoes! Back then we wrapped our feet in rotting tree bark! And considered ourselves lucky!

ANNCR: Nike Town. End of the 55 Freeway in Costa Mesa.

ED: You call that a freeway? In my day we travelled on rotting animal carcasses! And we liked it!

1-(800):
PRODUCT/MOUSE:

The Script

735 S.W. 20th Place   A Chris-Craft Station   Oregon Television, Inc.

P.O. Box 3401

Portland, Oregon 97208

Phone (503) 222-9921

:60 Radio Script "Moving Violations/
                                Outland"

Copywriter: Stephany L. Hale
             Promotion Producer

TONIGHT ON KPTV 12...THE CREATORS OF "POLICE ACADEMY" HAVE GONE
TOO FAR!   :05
    "You're in big trouble now, Mister!"   :01½
FELLING INNOCENT PEDESTRIANS....   :02
    Bowling ball hits pins SFX   :01
BURNING RUBBER ACROSS THE HALLOWED HALLS OF TRAFFIC COURT...   :03
    "Is this amusing or what?"   :01
    "Quiet!"   :0½
STRIPPING AWAY THE ROBES OF JUSTICE!   :02½
    "All right!"   :01½
BEWARE...   :01
    Screech/crash SFX   :01½
IT'S "MOVING VIOLATIONS"...   :02
    "Go ahead. Laugh."   :01
TONIGHT AT 8....   :01
    "What do you want, a special invitation?"   :01½

AND TOMORROW NIGHT ON TV 12...   :02
    "Somebody please help me. Please!"   :02½
SOMETHING IS WRONG ON THE OUTER FRINGES OF THE TWENTY FIRST CENTURY...   :04
    "Bingo."   :0½
    "Some kind of narcotic."   :01
    "It's an amphetamine."   :01
    "Makes you work like a horse."   :01
    "And then, it fries your brain."   :02
AND SOMEONE MUST STOP THE MADNESS!   :02½
    "That stuff they're selling is killing people."   :01½
    "You've been a very busy Marshal." "Yea, you proud of me?"   :02½
    "That can be very dangerous."   :01½
SEAN CONNERY FACES A FUTURISTIC "HIGH NOON" IN "OUTLAND"...   :03½

TOMORROW NIGHT AT 8, "OUTLAND". AND TONIGHT AT 8, "MOVING VIOLATIONS",
BOTH, ON KPTV 12!   :06

SCRIPT EIGHT

127

Maxey
Radio 60

MAX493 "Surprises"

I keep on getting surprises!
I TOLD you I was going to buy a Corolla from Bill
Maxey Toyota in Huntington Beach. And I did. And I
keep on getting surprises. Like on my last tank of
gas. City Driving. 30.7! That bippin' around town,
stop and go. And the shifting is a dream unto itself.
It sorta -- tracks, finds its own way. I didn't order
anything special, but I've got a fantastic radio. I
told Bill Maxey about all my surprises. That was a
mistake. He said he'd send me a bill! So far, he
hasn't.
But this is what you get from Bill Maxey Toyota in
Huntington Beach: Satisfaction PLUS surprises.
And still -- No Dealer Prep Charges.
No add-ons that can bump a car's price 3-or-4 hundred
to a thousand dollars. Not at Bill Maxey Toyota in
Huntington Beach. On Beach Boulevard, half-way between
the San Diego Freeway and the blue Pacific.
Enjoy your surprises. Tell your friends. (chuckle)
Just don't tell Bill Maxey.

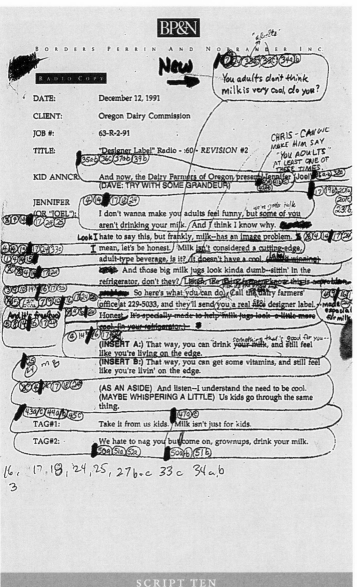

BP&N

BORDERS PERRIN AND NOLRANDER INC.

RADIO COPY

DATE: December 12, 1991

CLIENT: Oregon Dairy Commission

JOB #: 63-R-2-91

TITLE: "Designer Label" Radio - :60 - REVISION #2

KID ANNCR: And now, the Dairy Farmers of Oregon present Jennifer (Joel)
(DAVE: TRY WITH SOME GRANDEUR)

JENNIFER
(OR "JOEL"): I don't wanna make you adults feel funny, but some of you aren't drinking your milk. And I think I know why. Look I hate to say this, but frankly, milk has an image problem. I mean, let's be honest. Milk isn't considered a cutting-edge, adult-type beverage, is it? It doesn't have a cool. And those big milk jugs look kinda dumb--sittin' in the refrigerator, don't they? Listen, the dairy farmers' So here's what you can do. Call the dairy farmers' office at 229-5033, and they'll send you a real nice designer label. Honest. It's specially made to help milk jugs look a little more cool (in your refrigerator).

(INSERT A:) That way, you can drink your milk, and still feel like you're living on the edge.

(INSERT B:) That way, you can get some vitamins, and still feel like you're livin' on the edge.

(AS AN ASIDE) And listen--I understand the need to be cool. (MAYBE WHISPERING A LITTLE) Us kids go through the same thing.

TAG#1: Take it from us kids. Milk isn't just for kids.

TAG#2: We hate to nag you but come on, grownups, drink your milk.

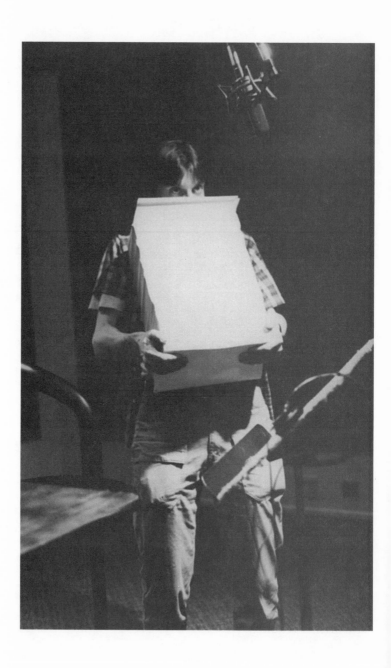

Narration

S IMPLY PUT, narration is the long form of voice-over. Scripts from a few pages to hundreds of pages are delivered by the narrator in a style that can best be described as...well, narrative. Educational videos, training films, informational slide shows, documentaries, motivational tapes, in-store displays, multi-image sales presentations, audio instruction manuals, and pre-recorded messages are all the domain of the narrator.

The best narration talent have a few characteristics in common:

- They all have durable voices that can tackle a twenty page script without tightening up, breaking down or wearing out. When you consider that even the best narrators have to do multiple pick-ups along the way, a twenty page script can easily become forty pages worth of reading.

- They have incredible consistency and control of their voices. A good narrator can go back ten pages, re-read a single paragraph and know exactly how to read it so it will edit cleanly into the rest of the script. This is a lot harder than it sounds. Remembering attitude, inflection, projection level, vocal tone and speed of delivery for the preceding and following paragraphs (so that the new insert will match perfectly) is no mean feat. Holding the same character for twenty pages isn't exactly easy, either.
- They practice clarity of diction. Nobody wants to listen to a sloppy speaker. Especially for several minutes.
- They possess an authoritative sound. Since narrators are usually cast in the role of teacher, tour guide, motivator, salesperson or corporate symbol, a certain command of the audience is necessary.
- They all have a fearless approach to complex copy and big, unfamiliar or highly technical words. Whether they understand what they are saying is inconsequential. They always sound like they understand.
- They are aware of their body position and presence in relation to the microphone. Once again, this is critical for consistency and matching reasons.
- They are quiet page turners, and the absolute best have little or no extraneous mouth noises. Since these would need to be carefully edited out later, an engineer faced with a lip-smacking narrator and a thirty page script to edit will probably be found crying in the corner.

One of the points mentioned above generates a fair amount of debate. Narrators need to be authority figures and, right or wrong, middle-aged men seem to monopolize this branch of voice-over work. An old line that's been bandied about through the ages is that, "Men like to listen to men — and so do women." It's this type of perception that undermines many women's attempts to break into the narration field. It's not that they lack authority, it's simply that in the past corporate producers have wanted that deep-voiced, powerful male announcer to carry their message. Corporate America still wants "the voice of God" to be their spokesperson and the overwhelming perception is that God sounds a lot like the Wizard of Oz, complete with cavernous echo, flames and green smoke.

As this paragraph is being written, however, things are changing. More and more large corporations are turning to the female spokesperson. This may be due to increased numbers of women in the boardrooms. It may be bowing to social or political pressures. It may simply be that the light bulb went on and somebody said, "Why not?" Whatever the reasons, women voice talent are finally getting a chance to play parts other than Mom, the brainless bimbo, the seductress or nosy old Mrs. Bevins from across the street.

Another reason why the traditional male narrator is losing his preeminent position is that we now operate in a world economy. We are finding that the American way of doing things isn't the only way. Female narrators are common in many countries and some of the overblown chest-pounding we Americans add to our presentations is considered needless and even laughable in other parts of the world.

In a recent example, a U.S. production company was producing a sales video for a large Japanese heavy equipment manufacturer. The producer had written a short script that gushed with the usual grandiose hype characteristic of American productions. The Japanese CEO objected. He wanted facts and figures and a long presentation that explained all aspects of their product. "American construction people aren't going to want to sit through an hour show with that much information," argued the producer. "It is all important!" replied the CEO. "Americans must learn patience."

Our perceptions are changing with the changing world. Things will not stay as they are, in life or in voice-over. For the moment, however, narration remains a male-dominated business.

Narration delivery is usually slower and more deliberate than commercial voice-overs. It has fewer vocal highs and lows, and most lines have a down inflection at the end rather than the up tone associated with commercials.

You don't need to bring along your big bag of emotions when doing narration. Very seldom will you be asked to get excited or morose. A common direction to narrators is to be "serious with pride." But just because narrators aren't usually fountains of emotion doesn't mean they aren't acting. Many of the best narrators are also fine actors. The often heavy-handed hyperbole found in narration scripts only sounds convincing when delivered with style. Good narrators learn vocal control and discipline that they use expertly for maximum impact.

There's an old gag about an actor so good he could read the phone book and make it sound interesting. Well, narration scripts can sometimes read like a phone book.

As with all voice work, the goal is to take the written words and make them sound like your own. With commercials, you benefit from the fact that copywriters are generally writing words for actors to read. In narration, however, writers are writing words for specific audiences to hear — audiences such as computer programmers, exhaust manifold installers, historians, veterinarians, supermarket check-out clerks, tax auditors or nuclear physicists. The goal is still the same, but achieving it can be challenging.

Try reading the following aloud:

NARR: The paracordum, a high density direct fusion unit, completes the optical collwheel assembly. When cauterized, the cab unit emits minute trailing elements while a thirteen gigahertz Bolstron controller eliminates extraneous casterization. QS2 rem studies have shown the compensators function best in low pressure dynamic situations. High pressure usage puts undue stress on L-Bar coupling and radiant sublimators. Cohesive hard copy printouts may be obtained through the AUTOMATA printer. Additional, long form, printouts are easily available by connecting the ZEROMATA printer. Attaching bellrung activators to quotient bearings can increase pro-stative output. In the event of increased vibration, fail-safe systems will disengage the primary boosters. Replacement of the boosters is a two person operation. Personnel with G8 or higher designation are required for this procedure. Replacement of swingtaps and modleboards may be done by operators of class G3 or higher. Access is available through the bi-valve port on the rear side of the unit. If you have questions, ask your supervisor for assistance.

If you can read this exercise with self-assured authority then maybe you're cut out for narration work. This example is total nonsense, but if you read it correctly, it sounds extremely important. That's the trick and the talent of narration.

Narrators often get another type of script that you may find more appealing:

NARR: Water. Clear, fresh, and life-giving to the crops of the Alacola Valley.

Rushing ever onward to the sea, the waters of the Minset River visit this lush valley to replenish the soil and color the land. Yellow citrus, green vegetables, blueberries and ruby-red fruit checkerboard the landscape in brilliant hues.

Farmers, who have tended this land for generations, move from field to field inspecting size, calculating weight and measuring progress.

Progress is slow. But only with time can the flavors of the Alacola Valley reach perfection. And it's perfection that the Alacola Valley is all about.

The possibility of an early frost, the likelihood of invading insects, and the consequence of even three extra days of rain weigh heavily on the minds of the land's caretakers.

But today is glorious, and worry will wait until tomorrow.

This is the more poetic form of narration. Did you spot some direction words? How about "fresh", "clear", "lush", "slow" and "glorious" for a start?

Narration

Narration scripts are often broken up into blocks that correspond to visual images. Sometimes a single word, such as "water" at the beginning, will stand alone. In the final production, long segments of music, sounds, visuals or other voices may interrupt the narration. Narration helps tie a production together and gives the piece a solid base on which to build. All the more reason for consistency on the part of the narrator.

Narration can initially be more profitable than commercial voice work. The session payment rates for "non-broadcast" productions are initially higher, but there are no use cycles or residual payments. In regular commercial work, you are paid for each 13-week cycle that the spot is on the air. Once you've been paid for a narration, however, it can be used forever.

Narrators on vacation are often surprised to run across a slide show exhibit with a narration track they recorded twenty years ago. They shouldn't be — some producers take the "forever" condition quite seriously. It's important to keep that in mind as you read your narration script. You may be associated with its subject matter for a long, long time.

If you pursue a narration career, you'll find that the producers who hire narrators and the producers who hire commercial actors are often different people. Usually, audio/visual producers, filmmakers and corporate "in-house" production departments are the leading buyers of narration talent. For the most part, these producers don't make radio and television spots. Talent for commercials tend to get hired by commercial producers and advertising agencies. These people don't often make slide shows or instructional videos.

Because of this, you may wish to make a separate demo tape of narration samples and deliver it to the most likely customers for that service. Another option is to make your demo tape two-sided, with commercial work on one side and narration on the other. If you choose this option, make sure the tape is clearly labeled.

Being successful in the voice-over business is difficult. Being successful in the narration portion of that business is even harder. Not only does narration work take a certain level of ability, it also comes with certain ingrained attitudes as to how it's supposed to be done. Character voices, women, young people, and older talent all have difficulty finding fame and fortune in narration. This is by no means a reason to abandon your dreams. If narration is your goal, you will need to pursue it with a little extra vigor. Practice by reading magazine articles, encyclopedia entries, instruction booklets, and repair manuals out loud. Try to develop that confident, authoritative sound that producers want. If you have trouble gaining authority, shoot for sincerity.

If nothing else, you'll improve your reading skills and build your self-confidence. And, of course, from a personal standpoint, reading a repair manual will never be quite the same.

Here are a couple more narration scripts to try:

Narration

CARE OF YOUR CAT
VIDEO NARRATION

(music up and under)

They are hunters, with muscles taut, and eyes fixed
on their intended prey.

They are gentle, with fluid movement and a sensitive
touch.

They are regal, with a lineage that goes back to
worshiped ancestors during the time of the Pharaohs.

They are introspective, aloof, unpredictable,
affectionate, comical and mischievous.

They are cats.

During the next few minutes, we'll take an in-depth
look at the animal that has become the number one
pet in America. An animal whose image conjures up
everything from majesty to bad luck.

(music up for titles)

Everyone it seems, owns a cat, yet we often wonder
if anyone truly *owns* a cat. Unlike the dog, cats
have a loner quality about them, often preferring
their own company to that of others. They stake out
their territory, choose favorite spots, and always
follow the sun.

Cats appear to sleep through much of the day, but these periods of sleep are usually of short duration. At the slightest sound they awaken to survey the situation. If all is well, they return to slumber while their ears remain constantly vigilant. Cats drop off into a deep sleep quickly, thus allowing them to get needed rest during their "cat naps."

When awake, cats tend to be alert and observant. They are attracted by small movements, warmth and new objects in their environment.

Cats are not all alike. When a new object is placed in their world, some cats will inspect it instantly. Others approach with caution. Still others will simply mark the object as their personal property and move on.

Despite their sometimes aloof demeanor, cats can be very affectionate. They can bond with humans in much the same way as dogs. Humans who provide a regular source of food are naturals for bonding. Cats show affection in a variety of ways. One of the best known is through purring.

Narration

Freightliner Trucks
Multi-Image Narrative Script

VISUAL/SFX	NARRATOR
Black screen, gradual lit with silhouettes, Morning, light, and dawn.	There is a price to be paid for the American dream.
As suggested.	It is a price built into the fields that feed us.
	The forests that shelter us.
	Into the power of our waters.
	And the riches of our mines.
	It is a price as inseparable from the abundance of America as is its beauty, diversity and grandeur.
Lightning flash, peal of thunder.	It is a price paid here.
As suggested.	Across the gauntlet of storm and blizzard of the

	Great Plains. Here. On the savage passes of the Rocky Mountains.
	Or here. In the no-man's lands of the seething Southwest deserts.
Grand Coulee	We have tapped America. But we have not tamed her. We have built fences and fortifications…
Reflecting glass towers	sealed ourselves in great jeweled cities of glass and neon…
Jumble of wires,	piped power to our homes and thrown pictures through the air.
Sequence of truck growling and winding over the road, towards the camera,at dusk.	But still, our cargoes must move across hostile frontiers…
	move as they have for centuries across the unimaginably vast and the unpredictably wild.

Where catastrophe still
stalks the mountains,

and calamity haunts the
plains.

To transport in America
is to be tested by its
immensity.

To deliver its riches is
to defy the distances.

...surmount the boundaries...
survive the extremes.

Segue. Faces behind
the wheel, dissolving
in and out of
rugged passing scenery.

And still, there are those
who follow the call. No
road is too hard, too long
or too lonely that there's
not a man to handle it.

Segue c.u.'s
of truck against loads.

No load is too heavy, too
hazardous or too demanding
that there's not the means
to haul it.

It is a tale told too
seldom, but told best by
Freightliner...the story of
those men and machines

to whom the impassable is
a challenge and the
impossible an opportunity.

It is they who deliver the
promise… who pay for the
American dream…

Theme logo… up "Magnificent Seven" theme.	Those Magnificent men… and their Efficient Machines.
Dissolves of ad comps.	It is a tale ripe for the telling in the trying times ahead… when heroes are too few and quality too rare. It is a composite of American faces and places and cargoes. A portrait of latter-day wagon masters lashing three hundred, four hundred horses and half the momentum of a locomotive, down super- highways and ribbons of road.
Construction trucks and environments, dissolving to	It is the story of human stamina and machine endurance. Of men who

appropriate ad comps.	move mountains, twenty tons at a time. Of vehicles whose burden is the very bedrock of progress. It's a belly full of dirt and a lung full of dust. It's truck landings lacerated like craters of the moon. It's the shudder of the machine under the sudden impact of a seven-ton shovelful of rubble.
Logging. Ditto.	It's the story of the loggers… thundering down the one-lane washboards of the Northwest woods, enough timber for ten houses strapped to their backs… ambushed by boulders and potholes… listening to the pounding of eighteen tires… listening with their ears… listening with their palms on the wheel, with their feet on the floorboards. No time for trouble: there are schedules to meet, quotas to be made.

CHAPTER 12

Animation Voice-Overs

A S WE GET INTO the more specialized forms of voice-over acting, it's important to remember that the job opportunities become limited. The animation voice market is very small. There is a solid pack of very good professionals doing most of the work, with lots of highly-talented newcomers waiting in the wings. This is not meant to discourage you from pursuing this career, however. It can be stimulating, fun, profitable and it can give you creative opportunities found nowhere else in show business. Just go into it with your eyes wide open and your perseverance stockpiled.

Every voice you do is a "character" voice in one form or another. An announcer, the girl next door, Dad, the shoe store clerk, a waitress or any parts you're asked to play in regular spots are just as much of a character as playing a cartoon hippopotamus. The difference is the former characters all have voices you can find in real life, whereas the hippo voice comes from the Land of Make Believe.

Animation is all around us — in commercials, on movie screens, at your local video store and in prime time. There is even an all-cartoon cable network. The largest concentration of animation is found on Saturday morning TV. The vast majority of these programs are produced by just a handful of production companies. You may be familiar with the names Hanna-Barbera, Warner Brothers, Disney, Filmation, Jay Ward and others. The actors at the top of the animation voice business usually work for companies such as these on a regular basis. They tend to work in teams specially assembled by the show producer to fill all the voice parts needed for a particular show. The number of characters can often exceed the number of actors, so some performers provide multiple voices within the production. This ability to create various vocal characters is a distinct advantage in animation voice-over.

In regular commercial voice work, you can develop a single style (often described as having "one act"), and be so good at it that you'll never need to do anything else. In animation, however, versatility is key. If you can do a wide range of characters in many shows, you will reap the benefits of regular work and increased financial reward.

In cartoons, the artwork generally isn't started until after the voice is recorded. Exceptions to this rule are animated series that are originally produced in one language and later dubbed into another. In traditional animation, however, the visual action is drawn based, in a large part, on the vocal action of the talent. Sometimes

148

live actors are filmed acting out the scene so animators can reproduce their movement and timing. Voice actors have even been filmed while recording their lines to help the artists create facial expressions. In short, the voice talent has a lot to do with how the animated character will sound, look and act.

One of the greatest character creators of all time was Mel Blanc, who provided virtually all the voices for the classic Warner Brothers cartoons from the 40's through the 80's. Bugs Bunny, Yosemite Sam, Elmer Fudd, Daffy Duck and Tweety Pie were just some of characters he created. Mel is credited on the cartoons as providing "voice characterization" because he supplied more than just a voice — he created a character.

A few years ago I had the opportunity to record Mel Blanc as he became a head of lettuce sitting in a crowded refrigerator. The project was a TV spot using the process of stop-motion animation. Stop-motion is a form of animation which uses three-dimensional objects rather than drawings. The objects are moved slightly for each frame of film so that they have movement in the finished product.

Because no film had been shot and the head of lettuce prop was still being constructed, Mel's only view of the character was from a rough drawing of the commercial. This type of drawing is called a "storyboard," and it's a condensed visual representation of what the producer wants the finished ad to look like. We've recreated the first couple frames of the storyboard to give you an idea of what Mel saw.

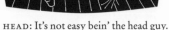

HEAD: It's not easy bein' the head guy.   You gotta be fresh… around here.

Before I tell you what Mel did, let's go through a little of the thought process for finding the character in you.

How big should the voice be? Well, we know that our character is inside a refrigerator so he's probably not a giant. The point-of-view of the camera is about 3 to 4 feet away. This isn't quite a close-up where an intimate sound might apply, nor is it a "wide shot" from far away where you might need to yell. From these clues we might deduce that a normal projection level with a full voice might be a good place to start.

What color is the character? Let's say that this head is pretty much lettuce-colored. Maybe the artists will make him a little brighter green just for the sake of television. Does green have a sound? Not sure? Well, would you say that green sounds different from red? If you were asked to use some adjectives to describe the color green, what would they be? How about *fresh*, *alive*, and *growing*? On the other hand, how about *inexperienced*, *shy* or *queasy*? It's okay not to know the answer right now. It's more important to get your imagination working and begin developing some vocal options.

What other qualities can we see in our head of lettuce? It's round. Round definitely has a sound. In fact, just saying the word "round" has a round sound. Does the lettuce look intelligent? It is a "head," after all. Is this a friendly lettuce? Does he look energetic or laid-back? And is he a he or is he a she?

The point here is that a drawing doesn't just lie on the page. By asking questions such as these, you can learn a lot about who this character is and how you might start a vocal characterization. The best voice talent go through this kind of mental process in a matter of seconds.

I mentioned earlier that you're trying to create vocal options for your director. As you present some of these options, it's helpful to explain why you have considered each voice. For example, you might say something such as, "I could do kind of a round voice like this, since the character is so round." Say the line in character. This puts the demonstration and the reasoning behind it together. Give the example quickly, then go on to your next voice option saying something such as, "Or...well, you know...he's really very green so...he could be kinda...well... ummmm...shy. I mean...if that's okay with you." Then move to your next option until you run out of ideas or the director stops you. Of course, you can use the actual copy from the spot to demonstrate your voices as well.

All this assumes that the director wants options. It's possible that he or she might have a particular sound in mind right from the start. If this is the case, don't start off the session by "playing" with the character. It's best to give the director what he wants first and save the options for later. In most situations, you'll get a chance to present your ideas at some point in the session.

Okay, let's pretend that I'm the director and I want

some options on this head of lettuce character. Ask yourself the questions we've discussed and give me four good voice characterizations. After you feel your vocal presentation is satisfactory, read on.

HERE'S A NEW storyboard and a new character. You'll need to come up with your own questions this time. When you're ready, I want you to present three well-conceived vocal options. Oh, and by the way, I don't want this character to sound anything like your lettuce character. Try going through the whole process in less than two minutes. GO!

VOX: Hey! What's a plant to do?   VOX: Where's the sunscreen?

How did it go? Do you feel pleased with the results? Did you picture a real plant that lives in your home or out in your garden? Did you adapt your read to reflect the changes that occur to the plant? Did your plant have an accent? How about vocal placement? Did any of your characterizations come from your chest, your throat or your nose? A flower with hay fever might have been an interesting character. With animation voice-over, you have free rein to try anything. Experiment. Try more physical things such as standing on your tip-toes, puffing up your cheeks, holding your nose and squeezing your throat. The best part about animation is that nobody thinks this type of behavior is silly or abnormal. I mean, if you can't have fun being a cartoon, when can you?

You can find characters in magazines, art museums and comic books. There are animated and "live action" (the opposite of animated — using real people) characters on billboards, Christmas wrapping paper and cereal boxes. And don't forget the inanimate objects all around that could have voices. The lamp on the table, the exercise bike in the basement, the dictionary in the bookshelf or the can of hair spray in your bathroom. With this many sources of inspiration, you can practice voice characterization all the time.

Now let's get back to the head of lettuce and I'll tell you what Mel Blanc did with it. He simply did what you just did. After a quick scan of the storyboard, Mel offered three voice options to the director. The director ruled out one, but asked Mel to run through the whole script "on mike" trying both the remaining voices. After a couple takes of each, one characterization proved to be the favorite and the session proceeded until the best take was "in the can." The entire process from the moment Mel walked in the door until the time he left took less than forty minutes.

This was just a thirty-second TV spot. What about other forms of animation? Do the same techniques apply? One of the best ways to find out is to ask a few animation voice-over professionals. So I gathered five very talented actors together to relate their experiences and share their insight into the world of animation and voice-over in general.

MICHELE MARIANA started her career in Missoula, Montana. Her multitude of voices have been heard on hundreds of radio and television commercials as well as on Public Broadcasting's *Reading Rainbow* and Nickelodeon's *Rug Rats*. Michele has been the obnoxious Wilshire Pig and the innocent Little Prince for Will Vinton's Claymation® studios and once provided twenty-six voices for a single animated production. Sesame Street characters Gloria Globe and Cecile Ball are voiced by Michele. She was featured in both the New York stage version and Oliver Stone's movie version of *Talk Radio* where, quite naturally, she played voices on the phone.

RUSS FAST's list of voices is endless. He's been hired to play such diverse characters as The Lone Ranger, Tonto, a couch, a dime and several dogs. One of his favorite characters was a monster in the cartoon *Grafoons* who talked a lot but never said an intelligible word. Russ also does extensive narration recording and acts as on-camera spokesman in many industrial videos. Russ spent five years in New York City where he worked off-Broadway as both an actor and director.

MARY MC DONALD-LEWIS got interested in voice-over as a theater arts student in Sacramento, California. She moved to Los Angeles where she became the voice of Lois Lane on *Superfriends* and Princess Goleeta on *Galtar and the Golden Lance* for Hanna-Barbera, Lady Jaye on *G.I. Joe* for Marvel, Maven on Warner Brother's *Batman* as well as Mom on Danger Production's *Things That Go Bump In The Night* for ABC. One of the hardest-working people in show business, Mary has provided voices for lots of animated little boys and animals, but she particularly enjoys playing strong female action hero characters.

VICKY VOSE, a native of Portland, Oregon, says she got started in voice-over because she was short. "People thought if you were short you could do children's voices," she explains. As a matter of fact, Vicky could do children's voices and many others as well. Throughout her career, she has been called upon to provide such voice characterizations as a clam, a lemming and a generic drug. With an extensive background as both a performer and director of musical theater, Vicky specializes in character singing. As for versatility, she was Olive Oyl for *Talking ViewMaster* and once tap danced in toe shoes on the infamous *Gong Show*.

TODD TOLCES grew up on Long Island in New York. Pursuing a radio career he eventually worked his way to Berkeley, California and later to the Pacific Northwest. Vocally, Todd has played everything from the Easter Bunny to Doctor Victor Frankenswine to Saint Peter for Will Vinton's Claymation® specials. For *The California Raisins* cartoon show, Todd played group manager Rudy Bagaman, Filbert and Sir Garlic. Never afraid to experiment, Todd voiced a space alien for Bugle Boy kids clothes and portrayed former president Ronald Reagan in the stage production of *Rap Master Ronnie*.

Those are the participants. Each with different perspectives and experiences. Only five actors, but a warehouse full of characters.

How did you get started doing character voices?

TODD "I probably started when I was watching cartoons as a child, and I started imitating my favorite cartoon characters, much to the horror of my parents. I thought that would be the best job in the world. Voice work became the natural evolution of all the screwball charac-ters I wanted to do from my childhood."

MICHELE "That childhood thing is true. All the kids in the neighborhood hung out together in the summer, and we'd start a story game at the beginning of the summer and carry it all the way through. Everybody would play all these different characters and do all these different voices, and I usually wound up telling stories at night. At the time it was no big deal, but now…Boing!"

RUSS "I started when someone who knew me as an actor encouraged me to do some character voices for commercials, which evolved into announcing, which evolved into animation voices."

Where do your characters come from?

TODD "I think some come from people we've met, some come from movies we've seen, commercials we've heard. I think voice actors are like sponges who suck up inspiration from everywhere. We've been blessed with the ability to do a wide variety of voices, and every day that goes by is an opportunity to suck in another voice. You want to do some character study? Go down to the bus station and hang out for an hour and listen."

MARY "I think I take sides of myself. Initially, I may pick it up from someone else, but I package it through myself. I need to find that person in me."

RUSS "I've been a mimic all my life. Whenever I've heard an accent or dialect or something that intrigued me, I wanted to see if I could do it. Often times it doesn't take for a long time, but when it does take, I have it for-ever. I know that's true of Michele who is still able to do some voices that she did when I first met her years ago…"

TODD "...And Russ is still trying to mimic them."

MICHELE "For me it's a combination of sources. A lot of times when I'm working on a character for a play, I hear the voice first. I guess I've always been a sound-oriented person. Often it's just a facet of yourself that relates to the character and finds a voice or finds a sound. It depends on the moment really."

VICKY "My voices are just me. Many times they are the people I don't get to be, or people I would want to be but can't because they wouldn't be socially acceptable."

If you get a script and it just says "dog" for a character description, do you develop a detailed mental picture of your character as well as a voice?

RUSS "For me, I like to find a mind set. It's a game I've played since I was a kid. If I were a dog, what kind of dog would I be? I do the voice of my own dog at home because he can't talk for himself. About the only thing I ask in a session is, "Where do you want the pitch?""

VICKY "Yea, it's just a little cartoon right in my head. The characters just come. I don't have to think about them really. They're all drawn and complete little creatures...or inanimate objects like a generic drug..."

MARY "Acetaminophen was my greatest challenge."

VICKY "At least you had a name. How do you get a picture of generic?"

Is an animation voice session different than a normal voice session?

TODD "You don't usually get a picture of the character when you walk into a regular voice session. There's not this drawing of 'announcer'..."

EVERYONE [*laughs*]

MARY "Yea, big guy with gray hair…"

RUSS "…about fifty…"

MARY "I think it compares to English riding in a ring versus endurance racing on a quarter horse. We can all go into a normal commercial session and look at the copy and say, 'Okay, I'm an archetype. I'm a dad. I'm a mom. I'm a this or that.' We've got thirty seconds to deliver a message so it's probably a broadly drawn character on the part of the copywriter with our personal touch added to it. With an animated session, the first difference is the sense of energy in the room. There's a wonderful collaborative feeling when you walk in. You gather around this crescent of microphones and it's like a high-wire act. You have to be sensitive to all the other actors and they have to be sensitive to you, so there's a need for lots of trust and sharing and timing and matching. It's harder. But more fun."

Most animation sessions are done with an ensemble of very good actors. Do you find it to be at all competitive?

MICHELE "My experience is that the better the people, the more comfortable they are, and the more tickled they are about somebody who can play. I've never felt animosity or competitiveness at all. Usually everybody's so jazzed, it's really fun."

MARY "I haven't done a lot of on-camera work, but I've always wondered if voice actors are more generous than face actors. Is that true?"

MICHELE "I don't think you can make that broad a generalization. It depends on the person. I've worked with some great people on and off-camera. I've also worked with some butt-heads on and off-camera."

TODD "I was talking with another voice actor one day and I asked him if he did any on-camera work. By all appearances he certainly could have but he said, 'No, it's too competitive.' He was more comfortable knowing his next session was going to be a voice session and it was going to be fun."

MARY "Friendly."

TODD "When I went to my first cartoon session in L.A., I was very nervous. I was in awe of all these other people because they were really very, very good and even though I had faith in my own abilities, I was still nervous. After we had worked about an hour or so, I realized they were all very cool and comfortable with me and that, in turn, made me more comfortable. They did not look at me as the guy from out of town. They were very friendly. They just let their mouths do their talking for them."

MICHELE "Which is a good way to do it."

When you first approach a characterization, do you let out all the stops or do you start conservatively and work up from there?

RUSS "Whatever my first impression is, I go for it. If it's wrong, I can adjust. If the director needs to pull me back, that's fine. But holding back or being tentative is not going to help anybody, so I just go for it."

VICKY "It's always easier to pull back than it is to push forward."

MICHELE "If the director isn't exactly sure of what he or she wants and you give them a good strong characterization, it tends to put them at ease because they know that you're in control of your part of the job and can deliver for them."

RUSS "The times I've done animation voices, the directors have been fishing. They sort of had a general idea but they really didn't know what they wanted."

TODD "They usually have that general idea, but they are relying on you to fine tune it."

RUSS "Once I'm in the studio, I'm being paid, so what's to worry? Just go to work."

With all these imaginative people in one session, are the scripts followed strictly or is there a lot of improvisation?

TODD "Depends on the director."

MARY "I think generally they're pretty strict because of the storyboarding."

MICHELE "It depends on the kind of job. I know that on some of the Claymation® stuff, I've been able to develop characters and dialogue as we went along."

TODD "But I think that for traditional cartoons the script is written a certain way for certain reasons. And because time is money, everyone's usually trying to get it done quickly, so you tend to follow the script."

MARY "For a show I've just been working on, I was sticking pretty close to the script, but one of the actors was going wild with ad libs. The directors were loving it, so one of the other actors threw in an ad lib line at the end. The directors liked it so much, it's become a button for the show. Because he took a risk. I'm sure he had permission, but other times doing that can really screw it up."

TODD "If it doesn't work, it doesn't work. I think we actors have to have hides of steel. The director has to be able to say, 'Look, read the script. Just read the script!' and we have to say, 'Okay, I certainly will.'"

How hard is it to get to the top of the animation voice-over profession?

TODD "There are a handful of people who work every-day in Toon Town. They do one session in the morning and one in the afternoon and they make lots of money."

MARY "But that's the bailiwick of only a handful of people."

TODD "And it truly is just a handful of people. With the largest pool of great talent in southern California, it still comes down to just a few people who do most of the work."

RUSS "In New York, one of the top voice talents sat down with me and explained how it works there. He said there are about twenty people who do ninety-five percent of the work. And they tend to specialize. There are guys who only do up endings, guys who only do down endings and guys who do "trick" voices, which is what we do. Unless you earn your way onto that imaginary list, you're not going to work. You may get some smaller accounts or an odd job here and there, but you're not going to make the big money. It took this guy twelve years to get on the list and he's a great talent. Now he does ten gigs a year and makes over a hundred thousand dollars. But he only does up endings."

MICHELE "My experience in New York was very different, real positive."

MARY "I think that one of the reasons the top pool doesn't expand much goes back to the ancient roots of theater where actors were a troupe. They were looked down upon and were turned away from hotels. They just had to hang together and that united them. The animation community has a lot to do with relationships.

Opportunities don't happen so much through auditions as they do because someone likes you and knows you can deliver the goods consistently. It's sort of an old-fashioned thing. Now occasionally someone comes knocking at the door demanding admittance, and they won't quit pounding until someone lets them in. That was me fifteen years ago. But it is rare."

MICHELE "On a strictly business level, these people have a product to turn out. There are big bucks involved, so they have to turn to actors who they know can deliver in a timely fashion."

TODD "There are more opportunities today than there were in the 70's, however. There are more videos being made. There are more books on tape, more CD ROM projects, whatever. But I think in every town there is an inner circle and an outer circle of voice talent."

MARY "And the inner circle works first."

MICHELE "If you're in that inner circle and a producer wants to hire you, but for some reason you can't do the job, the producer will often take your recommendation. That's another way to bring new talent into the circle and it's nice to be in that position. Of course, the new talent has to earn the right to stay."

What do you tell people who may be afraid to move away to the big city to pursue this career?

MARY "The voice business is full of people who come from teeny, teeny towns."

MICHELE "A lot of people complain that it's just too competitive in the big markets. Hey, it's competitive everywhere. You've got yourself to offer and you're just as valid where you are as anywhere else. Instead of worrying what's out there, concentrate on what you can contribute and focus on competing with yourself and refining your skills. Don't worry about all that other stuff, because that can stop you in a town of five hundred or five million."

MARY "I think people should totally go for it. Throw caution to the winds, figure on being poor for a while and never not do it just because it entails putting yourself in a box and moving."

RUSS "Those of us who've gone off to the big cities and later move back home are often ridiculed. People say, 'What went wrong? Why are you back here?' I just say, 'I don't see you putting your butt on the line. Why don't *you* go do it?' That's the message. If you really want to do this, you just have to go. And if you don't make it, so what?"

MARY "And if it stops feeling good, get out."

MICHELE "Some people act like if you step across a borderline, the old state or country or whatever disappears. You're just expanding your frame of reference and your territory. You're adding another wing to the house."

TODD "It takes courage. And maybe a little stupidity. The risk is high that you will not succeed. But that isn't the reason not to go."

VICKY "You know, sometimes it's scary to go away to the big city seeking your fortune. But then, sometimes it's scary to just stay where you are."

What can you tell me about casting directors?

TODD "In L.A., there might be eight or ten of them working regularly. They are a go-between who answers to the person who hires, so they better bring them credible talent."

MARY "As a young actress first going out with my sad

little head shot and stuff, I found on-camera casting directors to be abrupt, rude and…abrupt and rude. That about covers it. Voice casting directors on the other hand, I have found to be nice and reassuring and friendly people. I think people who are attracted to voice, whether they're an animation director or casting director or agent who specializes in voice, do it because they have a love of voice and voice acting. There is a joy there that, in my experience, is missing from on-camera casters."

RUSS "Voice casters do tend to be more nurturing. They want you to succeed and they tend to help you. Whereas an on-camera casting director's job is to weed you out. They don't care if you're having a bad day. It's just *out*!"

TODD "Next!"

MARY "I tell this casting director story in the voice-over classes I teach. When I was first starting out in L.A., I kept pounding on the door of the best voice casting director in town and he shunned me and shunned me and shunned me. So I went home and I wrote this angry little letter saying, 'How dare you! I've got to become famous really fast here…*Arrrggg*.' And it's the one letter in my whole life that I had sense enough not to mail. As it turned out, I went on to have a long working relationship with the guy, so…"

VICKY "Once, I learned a casting director was holding a major animation audition in L.A. I only had a few hours notice and I was in Portland, Oregon at the time. But I did go purchase an airline ticket and flew down there, spent about two or three minutes in the booth and flew back home the same day. The experience was about what I thought it would be and it was a good one. Even though I didn't get the job."

How do you personally measure success?

RUSS "Most of the people who I started in the business with are not in the business anymore. I feel successful because I'm still doing what I love to do. I suppose I could be making much more money elsewhere, but I like making a living at this and that's what I do."

MARY "I agree that making a living at your craft is itself a success story. I also measure my success by knowing that my work is as honest as I can make it. I don't always care if I get the gig or not. If I feel good about what I did…that's enough. Job finished."

MICHELE "I've always been able to do things I believe in and stand by my ethics and sometimes say, 'No, thank you'."

VICKY "I've never thought if I was successful or not. It's like you go into the studio and do it, and it's a wonderful place where I enjoy being. Happiness. I guess that's a form of success."

TODD "I suppose I'm successful as long as people still want to use my voice for something. As long as people still call my agent and say, 'Get that guy,' and my peers consider me a good talent, that's success. None of us here are lighting up big cigars with thousand dollar bills or sipping a glass of cognac but…"

MARY "…but it's early."

What other types of jobs have you held in pursuit of your career?

EVERYBODY "Maid, maître d', nurse's aide, shoe sales-man, bartender, photo stylist, bus person, artist's model, costume designer, illustrator, newspaper delivery person, night club singer, waiter, radio announcer, writer…"

Do you have a favorite character you like to do?

TODD "I tend to like slapstick characters, characters who exaggerate everything. You can just hear their eyeballs flying out of their heads. They really allow me to stretch my voice."

RUSS "I like guys with really negative attitudes. Whiners. When I was in New York, I was in heaven. I could sit in a coffee shop and just listen to people talk. Some of them had fascinating ways of turning a phrase."

Do you all talk out loud to yourself?

EVERYONE "Yes!"

TODD "I compare it to working out in the gym. It's vocal exercise."

MICHELE "I talk out loud to myself so much that when I was learning to sign for Theater for the Deaf, I realized at the supermarket one day that I was signing to myself all the time. It was very funny and totally unconscious."

Do other people ever question the worth of doing this kind of work?

MICHELE "Sometimes it even comes from people in the industry, but usually not from people on our side of the glass. I think it's because people don't understand it. It's really a subtle and intricate mechanism. It's a very disciplined art form. There's a big difference between sitting around making funny sounds and creating a full-fledged character."

What advice would you give to someone getting started in the animation voice business today?

TODD "You've got to be able to read and write and

have a good grasp of language. And market yourself aggressively."

MARY "Most people just starting out are just too timid about marketing themselves."

TODD "Just having an agent and a head shot is not enough."

RUSS "You've got to have persistence. You never know when a contact is going to pay off. This happened to me in New York. I dropped off a tape at an agency and a year and a half later, they called me."

MICHELE "Another important thing is to learn to let it go. If you feel like you've done the very best job you can do, then let it go. There are so many factors determining whether you'll get the job or not. You just have to trust that it's always somebody's turn and eventually it will be yours."

TODD "Once that audition is done, cut it loose. Don't worry about it. Look forward to your next audition and don't just sit by the phone."

MARY "And be nice to everybody. First and foremost because it makes your life better, and secondarily because the guy who's delivering packages around town will be your agent in about four years."

TODD "Or that same guy is interning at the recording studio and he works his way up to being an engineer and one day some ad agency guy asks him who he'd recommend for some job and he mentions you."

RUSS "And remember, the audition you do today may be remembered six months from now for some other job."

MICHELE "Every time you're out there you are repre-senting the entire marketplace. The more solid talent on all sides of the microphone, the better for the whole community. If you didn't get a job and one of your fellow actors got it, that's still good. It means the work stayed here, and it doesn't mean that you aren't good. It just means that you were different and the producer couldn't use that difference at that moment."

Any final thoughts?

MARY "One of the things that I think is really consistent with voice actors and people who work in animation is that not one person among them takes it for granted. These people have worked so hard to get there that, when it comes, they give thanks every day. They never forget what a blessing it is."

And with that, I'd like to give thanks to these five talented people for their comments and candor. The industry itself is blessed to have them.

We'll finish this chapter with a few pages of script from a fanciful animated series. Try doing all the characters. Remember, this is animation so women can be men and vice-versa. Don't be afraid to stretch your vocal repertoire and most of all, have fun with it.

ANNOUNCER

First there was Tarzan of the Apes. Then came Lawrence of Arabia, Nanook of the North and Sergeant Preston of the Yukon. Now, across a galactic time warp and through the black hole of your imagination comes Commander Joshua Skum and his Earth Force Five. Fighting crime throughout the galaxy, bringing evil doers to justice and making space a safe place to live. It's… SKUM, OF THE EARTH! We join our hero on board a float in the Malentorpe

---

Days Parade on the planet Cilivac Six...

SKUM
Don't tell me about public service, Doctor Penny.
I'm knee deep in public service.

DR. PENNY
But Josh, think about all the good PR we're generating.

SKUM
[groan]

DR. PENNY
The people of Cilivac Six will now look upon Earth
in a whole new light.

SKUM
They can't even see Earth from here.

DR. PENNY
Wave to the people, Josh.

SKUM
Hi there, good to see you. Glad you could make
it...You know, Doc, I'd just like to see our little
space patrol turn a profit now and then. I mean the
ol' Mother Ship doesn't run on pride.

DR. PENNY
I know.

SKUM
We've only got enough Proton Propellant to get us a
couple million light years from here. And that's
like nowhere.

DR. PENNY

I calculate that, with a good coast, we can make
the Kabar Star System.

SKUM

With a good coast?

DR. PENNY

Well, if my calculations are correct, we'll run out
of ProtoPro about seven hundred and thirty five
thousand kilometers from the planet Atross.

SKUM

Atross!!? That place is a dump.

DR. PENNY

That's a little harsh, Josh.

SKUM

I mean it, the planet is a dump. It's a planetary
landfill. For centuries, neighboring planets dumped
their garbage in a remote part of space. After a
while, the pile of junk grew so massive that it
produced its own gravitational field. Everyone kept
adding more trash until it became the largest
planet in the Kabar Star System. Eventually, the
original planets were totally depleted of natural
resources. They had converted everything into
garbage...and all that garbage was now Atross. It
was a recycling gold mine. Well, they fought devas-
tating wars over it until only remnants of once
proud civilizations survived. The last of them made
peace and went on to colonize Atross.

                    DR. PENNY
Amazing! Have you been there?

                     SKUM
I've been to the capital, Atross City. It's a dump,
too. But I have to admit, it's a fascinating place.

Styrofoam buildings, cardboard cars and the streets
are paved with beer cans.

                    DR. PENNY
Sounds wonderful. We'll leave for Atross on Tuesday
morning.

                     SKUM
Why wait for Tuesday?

                    DR. PENNY
Oh, I forgot to mention that a Malentorpe Days
Parade lasts for three days.

                     SKUM
What???!!!!

                    DR. PENNY
Wave at the people, Josh.

                   ANNOUNCER
So it's off to Atross for Commander Skum and his
crew: Doctor Penny, Chief Engineer Molly Knight,
co-pilot Theodore Savrus and the mystical Doriana.
Separately, a pretty odd lot. But together, they
are known as Earth Force Five. Pride of the galaxy,
guardians of peace, model citizens and non-smokers.

Unfortunately, at the moment, Doctor Penny's calculations have left them a little short.

MOLLY
Commander, we've just exhausted our ProtoPro reserve.

SKUM
Doctor, you said…

DR. PENNY
I said we'd need a good coast.

SKUM
We can't coast all the way to Atross from here. We'll miss it by a million kilometers.

DORIANA
One million seventeen point two five eight kilometers.

SKUM
Thanks Doriana, I needed that.

THEO
We're starting to drift.

SKUM
Well, there's only one way to stop that. Whose turn is it to get out and push?

MOLLY
I think it's your turn, Mon Capitán.

SKUM

Great Gollyhorns!!

ANNOUNCER

So Commander Skum dons his pressurized suit and starts to exit the crippled spacecraft. However, unbeknownst to the Commander, the other end of his umbilical cord (normally attached to the ship's framework) is instead wrapped around a loaf of day-old French bread. Who could have done such a dastardly deed? And what are the consequences for our hero? Stay tuned...

SKUM (OVER RADIO)

Do you read me, Theo?

THEO

Loud and clear.

SKUM

How far off course are we?

MOLLY

Seven degrees. I'd say sixty or seventy good pushes should do it.

SKUM

Swell. Here goes. [Big groan]

THEO

Good one.

DORIANA

Six point nine nine nine nine nine five degrees remaining.

SKUM

What?!!

MOLLY

Bad timing, Doriana.

DR. PENNY

Say, did anybody see a loaf of day-old French bread I had stored in the kitchen?

ANNOUNCER

No one has time to answer. The missing loaf of day-old French bread breaks in half, releasing Commander Skum into space.

SKUM

Aaaaaaaiiieeeee!!

THEO

What is it, Josh?

SKUM

My umbilical has come loose.

MOLLY

I told him to get that thing replaced at the last space port.

DR. PENNY

Quick, Molly, to the release chamber.

DORIANA

It's too late. The Commander has drifted beyond rescue range.

THEO
Josh, you know I can't come to get you without power.

SKUM
I know, Theo. It's not your fault.

THEO
You bet your life it's not my fault.

MOLLY
Bad choice of words, Theo.

SKUM
You're the engineer, Molly, invent some fuel or something.

DORIANA
Radio contact diminishing.

THEO
We're losing you, sir.

SKUM
Well, this is no time for messy good-byes.
Before I go, I just want to say to all of you that it's really been…

[radio static]

The STUDIO CONSOLE *or* BOARD *(above) is the "plumbing" that helps get your voice from the microphone to the recorder. It also allows the engineer to combine various audio tracks into a composite mix. Faders at the bottom control level. Other knobs and buttons control such things as equalization, panning, echo, monitoring and assignments. Many modern audio computer systems have consoles built in.* MICROPHONES *(right) come in many shapes and sizes. Their design dictates their use and each possesses a unique sound quality.*

CHAPTER 13

Introduction to the Studio

RECORDING STUDIOS can take many forms. They can be built in a home, in a high-rise office building, in a storage room behind a liquor store, or in a meticulously designed complex full of special touches of acoustical detail.

As varied as they are, you will probably notice a few basic elements in common.

A true recording studio is actually two rooms: a control room where the engineer and director work, and a studio room or BOOTH where you work. The rooms are separated by a wall with a viewing window and some-times a door. The control room is equipped with an audio mixing console or BOARD and recording machines such as tape decks, digital recorders or digital audio worksta-tions. The studio will usually have at least one microphone, a music stand or copy holder and a chair.

The rooms may be quite large or very small. They may

have wood paneling, acoustical foam, felt-covered fiber-glass, or old egg cartons covering the walls.

The control room may be filled with dozens of extra electronic devices for SIGNAL PROCESSING (a fancy way of saying sound altering). These devices can help the engineer make you sound like you're in an empty auditorium or in the shower. They can change your pitch, diminish sibilance, turn you into a robot, speed you up, remove certain frequencies from your voice, control your volume level, put you under water, suppress your breaths, roll off your highs, shelve your lows, push your mids (frequencies, that is), adjust your timing and compress your dynamics.

Some voice actors joke that, "With all this technology, who needs talent?" Well, the fact is, these amazing electronic processors are pretty useless without something to process. They can't change your accent or raise your projection. They can't do a thing about emphasis, emotion, style and believability.

In other words, they can't act worth a darn. The adage, "We'll fix it in the mix" is usually more an expression of desperation than preference. It's still much better to get a good performance from the talent and use editing and processors to aid the session, not rescue it.

In some of the more elaborate studios, you will notice structural features that make the room acoustically correct. For instance, the walls may be angled so that there are no parallel surfaces. There may be sound diffusers hung like panels from the ceiling or built into the back walls.

The glass window between the rooms is usually two panes with an air space between. This gap may be a few inches or a few feet. The idea is to isolate the rooms, sound-wise, from the world outside and from each other.

This can only be accomplished by mass and by air space. The walls of the studio can be made massive, but the window panes need the air space to make up for their lack of mass.

Will knowing this type of information make a difference in how you read copy? Well, it may help you understand your environment which may make you more comfortable which, in turn, may affect your performance.

The mixing console may be an overwhelming piece of electronics, full of many colorful buttons, knobs, lights and meters. Don't be intimidated. No matter how big it is, its main job is to channel your voice from the microphone to the recorder as accurately as possible. After you've left the studio, it will be used to combine the various elements of the production (voices, music, sound effects) into the final mix. It may be automated with computer-driven memory or operated manually. Mixing consoles can also be quite small, especially in these days of digital audio, where an entire console may be reduced to an image on a computer screen.

Don't judge a studio's abilities by the size of its board or the number of flashing lights. The true talent of the equipment is in the person who runs it. Talent, as far as this book is concerned, is a *human* thing.

A console is basically a series of component channels, each with an on/off switch, a volume control, a fancy set of bass & treble controllers called E.Q. (equalization), a panning POT (potentiometer) that allows the engineer to place audio parts to the left or right in a stereo mix, a switch that selects input from either a microphone or a machine, and output selectors that direct the audio signal to one or more desired destinations. Bigger consoles have more doodads, but this is the basic setup.

If you think of your voice as a flow of water, then the mixing console is simply the plumbing that moves it from place to place. If the console is the plumbing, then the speaker is the faucet and the recorder is the bucket that holds your performance until it's needed.

You are likely to see several speakers in the control room. Large speakers, also called MAIN MONITORS or MAINS, are mounted on or in the front wall. Smaller speakers called NEAR-FIELD MONITORS often sit atop the console. By listening to the various speakers, the producer and engineer can mix the production (that is, blend all the audio elements together) for the medium it's intended for. For instance, radio spots are best mixed on smaller speakers since they will ultimately be heard on radios which tend to have small speakers, while music or theatrical presentations need the big honkers. Motion pictures are often mixed in MIXING THEATERS. There will also be a set of speakers in the booth. These are used to play back sound to you and allow the people in the control room to give you direction via the TALKBACK.

The talkback is the system that lets the director and engineer talk to you between takes. Normally, a small microphone in the console picks up the voices in the control room and sends them to your booth speakers. The engineer or the director controls the talkback with the press of a button. The talkback should not be used during recording because the sound coming through your speakers will be picked up by your microphone and transferred to the recorder. If you are wearing headphones, the talkback can often bypass the studio speakers and transmit directly through your cans. There is no need to talk louder when the talkback is on. Always remember that the microphone is the ear of control room personnel. If they ever have trouble hearing you, the engineer will simply turn you up. The talkback is also used to give you the slate of each take. When the direction is over and it's time for you to read, the engineer usually says something like, "This is spot one, take twelve." The talkback will be shut off and you can begin when you're ready.

Recorders come in all shapes and sizes. Though they are becoming rare in studios, you may be recorded onto a reel-to-reel tape deck. You might be recorded directly to an audio or video cassette. These forms of recording are called ANALOG. Your voice causes a magnetic field to arrange tiny particles on the surface of the tape into a precise pattern. This pattern can later be "read" by the tape deck and translated back into sound.

DIGITAL audio doesn't really record sound at all. It records a complex series of numbers on the tape or onto the drives of a computer workstation. These numbers are later decoded into the sound that produced them in the first place. Digital systems can usually be spotted by their video screens and computer keyboards.

DAT (Digital Audio Tape) recording is sort of a cross between analog and digital. A DAT machine records digital information onto a magnetic tape. DAT recording is pretty much the standard in studios today.

Whether you're recorded by an analog or digital recorder should make no difference to your performance.

You may be surprised to see hard surfaces and high ceilings in the studio and control room. Most people think this would cause odd reverberation and "roominess" in the acoustics. A well-known studio designer once said that the idea is to control sound, not kill it. The image of a studio looking like a padded cell is a thing of the past. Studios need to have a certain "liveness" and audio character. They need to be quiet, which usually means keeping outside sounds out and inside sounds in. To accomplish this, studios are often physically detached from the rest of the building so that vibrations cannot transfer from room to room. This type of construction is called a FLOATING STUDIO. If it's built correctly, you won't feel any difference, but the sound isolation will be greatly improved.

This isolation is cause for what some talent call the *Fishbowl Syndrome*. You sit in a room looking out through a pane of glass at the rest of the world. You can see people talking in the control room but you can't hear what they're saying because they haven't switched on the talkback. Left alone in this unnatural environment, your mind starts to wander. What are they talking about in there? Are they lamenting their decision to hire you? Are they complaining about your performance? Are they trying to figure out how to get rid of you gracefully?

The answer is almost always *no*. They're probably just discussing some small production detail. In fact, it's often routine to leave the talkback off until all discussion is over and a clear direction is at hand.

Just the same, that fishbowl feeling tends to come over you. You are being critically observed and yet you're cut off from any reaction. Unless they let you in on the conversation, you don't know how you're doing and that can be unnerving. Only experience and self confidence can lessen its impact. Having another talent in the room doesn't hurt, either. Keep your mind on your performance and don't worry too much about what's going on in the control room. They're probably just ordering lunch anyway.

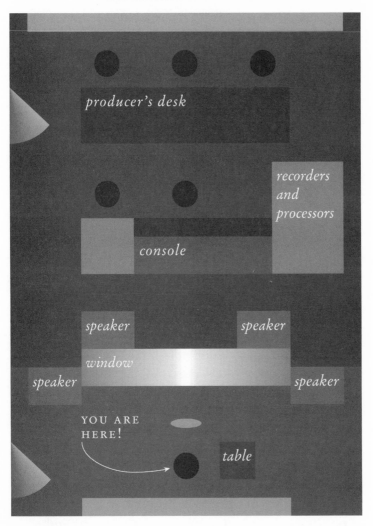

A COMMON STUDIO LAYOUT— *Studio designs vary widely, but many will follow this basic setup. In studios that do a lot of music as well as commercial voice recording, the talent booth may be much larger than the control room.*

You should be aware of a few technical aspects of studio operation.

Never, ever blow or yell into a microphone unless you've been instructed to do so. Studio microphones can be very expensive and very delicate pieces of equipment. Mikes can be PADDED electronically for loud sounds, but only by the engineer. You can seriously damage an unpadded microphone by giving it too much volume to handle.

A studio floor is often strewn with cables. Try not to walk or stand on any of them. If they are in your way, ask the engineer for assistance. Do not just move things on your own. You may as well let the engineer be the one who knocks over the music stand or pushes the boom through the window.

What's a boom? That's the large microphone stand that allows the mike to hang down from above. Do not hit or tap on a boom when its mike is HOT (turned on). The vibration could cause a loud noise in the control room. This goes for small mike stands as well.

Be careful of setting food or beverages near any electrical component. Some type of table or stand will probably be available, out of harm's way, for this purpose. It's always a good idea to ask the engineer if you can take such items into the booth in the first place. Studio policies vary.

If you wear headphones and like to have the level turned way up, be careful not to take them off near the microphone. A feedback loop can be created that can audibly hurt you, other talent, and those in the control room.

You've no doubt heard feedback before. It's caused when sound feeding into a microphone comes out a speaker and back into the mike. It produces a high screeching tone

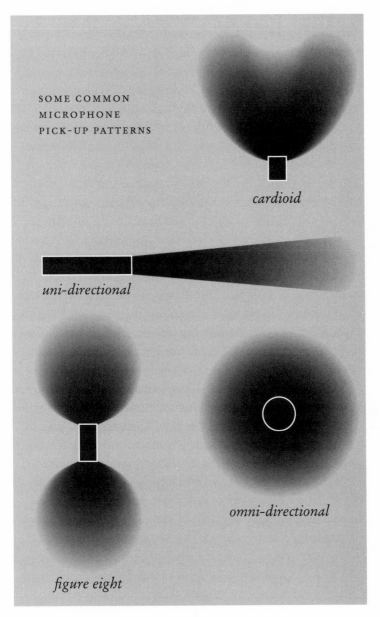

SOME COMMON
MICROPHONE
PICK-UP PATTERNS

cardioid

uni-directional

omni-directional

figure eight

of intense level. If you've ever been hit with feed-back through a set of headphones, you know how painful and potentially damaging it can be.

For the overly concerned, this may be another reason for not wearing cans. In most modern studios, however, there are built-in safeguards against feedback. By the way, it's a good idea to remove your headphones whenever cables are being plugged in or unplugged, and whenever live mikes are being moved. The bumps, pops and snaps associated with these actions can also be loud.

Obviously, equipment in the control room is off limits unless you've been invited to touch.

PRACTICING proper microphone technique shows true professionalism and enhances your performance.

The most common studio mikes might be cylindrical, square, round and flat. They can be as large as a half-gallon of milk, as long as a loaf of French bread and as small as a split pea. Each one has a unique audio quality and serves a specialized purpose. There are some mikes that are perfect for the high strings of a piano, while others are best for kick drums, acoustic guitars or, of course, voices. A good engineer will know which microphone to use. In some cases, the engineer may set up more than one mike to see which sounds better with your particular voice.

The area a microphone hears is called its PICK-UP PATTERN. Some mikes have a fixed pattern while others are switchable.

Most studio mikes you will run across have a CARDIOID pattern. This means that they pick up sound best in a heart-shaped area in front of the mike and reject sound from the rear. The cardioid pattern is popular because it allows for slight head movement by the talent without going OFF MIKE. Other mike patterns you may encounter include the FIGURE EIGHT which permits two people to face each other and use the same mike, the OMNI-DIRECTIONAL which picks up sound from all sides, and the UNI-DIRECTIONAL HYPER-CARDIOID, which is often referred to as a *shotgun* because of its long barrel.

A shotgun microphone is extremely directional. It picks up sound in a narrow band extending from its nose and rejects all other noise. You will often see these mikes used to pick up sound from more than six feet away. The fact that they must be pointed directly at the sound source makes their shotgun appearance a bit ominous. Many a nervous talent has felt intimidated looking down the barrel of a fully loaded hyper-cardioid.

Two other mikes are used more often in television applications, but also make infrequent appearances in the recording studio. The HAND-HELD mike has a special casing that allows you to hold it while preventing any hand movement from being heard. The LAVALIERE or *lav* is a small mike that can be hidden in your clothing, hung around your neck or pinned to your lapel. It is omni-directional and is used when you must be able to move around the room without changing your mike presence. In some cases, the lav is attached to a wireless transmitter that you carry in your pocket. This allows even greater freedom of movement with no cables dragging across the floor.

Most of the time, the studio mike will be attached to a stand or a boom and you won't have to worry about it. The engineer may choose to raise the microphone above your mouth to pick up more nasal clarity, lower it to hear more resonant chest sound, or pull it off to the side to lessen sibilance and prevent popped "P's".

Another device used to reduce the plosive "P" is the WINDSCREEN or WINDSOCK. This may be a foam piece that covers part of the mike or it may be a circular hoop of fine fabric placed in front of the mike. Windscreens are often used in outdoor recording situations where wind can be a significant problem.

You may also see BASS TRAPS in some studios. These are usually fabric-covered cylinders of varying height and diameter. They are set up in a room to remove extraneous low frequencies that may be generated by outside vibration, air conditioners or the room itself.

When you're ready to read, place your copy so you look straight ahead. Having to look down or up cuts off airflow and reduces breath control. It also makes it harder to place your mike correctly.

Remember that you're working inside the pick-up pattern of the mike. You can move slightly from side to side without changing your sound but you have limits. The mike is probably more sensitive to distance. If you lean back or move in on the mike, your presence will change. Your engineer will be keeping track of this but, unless you like doing things over, you should be aware of mike proximity and try to hold your position.

Mike pick-up patterns work in your favor in one important situation. Let's say you need to sneeze, or cough, or clear your throat. These sounds may be substantially louder than your speaking voice. By merely turning out of the mike's pattern, you can sneeze your head off and not hurt the folks in the control room. This is a simple and kind gesture on your part and will go a long way in showing your professionalism.

In a dialogue spot, the two talent will often be set up facing each other. This is done to take advantage of each microphone's pick-up and rejection patterns and to encourage eye contact between the talent. Three talent will usually be positioned in a triangle, four in a square and so on until the booth is too full to function properly. Talent in the same spot will sometimes be recorded separately and put together later. This is particularly true of spots where the talent do not interact. There may even be special circumstances when multiple interacting talent will work from separate rooms, or be PATCHED together from different cities.

One other aspect of studio design may be of interest to you. Many studios are equipped with light dimmers. Depending on the script, you may wish to adjust the lighting to set a proper mood. It never hurts to ask, if you think it will help your read. Remember that your comfort is important. Everyone in the session wants to get the perfect take on tape. Accomplishing that is everyone's concern.

Small, low-budget recording studios can be an interesting experience. Tales are told of broken headphones, poor air conditioning and no talkback systems. Some talent tell about places where they even had to run their own board during the session. Certain studios are oriented more to the music business than to the commercial world, so talent can find themselves crammed into booths full of synthesizer keyboards, drum kits, sheet music, miles of cable and curious odors.

Not all studios are built to be soundproof, either. I've heard of one studio that had to cease operation every time the radio at the pizza parlor downstairs got too loud, and another that was interrupted every time the studio phone rang or the toilet was flushed. The best advice is to take it all in stride and enjoy the ride.

You'll find that most studios are non-smoking facilities. In some, a smoking area is provided.

One unique session situation is the PHONE PATCH. This is where the talent and the director are in different locations and work together over telephone lines. You will need to wear headphones for this type of session. The director, who may be across town or across the country, calls the studio and is patched into the session. You'll be able to hear the engineer, the director and yourself over your headphones.

If regular phone lines are used, the director will hear your reads just like any normal phone conversation. After the session, the tape recorded at your studio is shipped to his or hers so the production can be completed.

If a digital phone line or a satellite is used, however, the director can be recording your performance directly at his or her studio, just as if you were in the next room. That's how clear these digital-based transmissions are. It's fun to think about your voice bouncing off some satellite out in space and being miraculously captured by a computer in another city. Pretty mind boggling stuff. Especially when you're speaking on behalf of Aunt Agatha's Fudge Brownies or Flusho Toilet Bowl Cleaner.

Every production — whether a quick low-budget spot for a used car dealer, or a multi-million dollar motion picture — has three stages: *pre-production, production and post-production*. The talent is usually only involved in the production stage.

PRE-PRODUCTION involves such things as budgeting, script writing, studio scheduling and casting.

Introduction to the Studio

POST-PRODUCTION is the term used to describe everything that happens to the project after the talent leaves.

A radio spot, for example, may require many hours of
additional work by the engineer and producer after your
lines have been recorded. First comes TAKE SELECTION,
or simply listening to all the reads and selecting which
takes are the best. The selected takes are then pulled from
the session master and edited together.

Appropriate music may need to be found. Music for
commercials comes either from production music libraries,
which are collections of pre-produced pieces in a wide
variety of styles, or it may be specifically written and
recorded for the spot. Similarly, sound effects can be
gathered from sound effect libraries or specially created.

All the parts are edited and layered together, each on its
own audio track. This process still tends to be called
"multi-tracking," even though many digital audio work-
stations don't really have tracks. When all the elements
are in place, the engineer sets volume levels for each track,
uses audio processing where needed and combines
the audio pieces into a composite product called the MIX.

Many professional voice actors never get to hear the final
product. They are quite satisfied simply knowing they
turned in a good performance and the check is in the mail.
Other talent like to get a copy or dub of the mix so they
can hear their work in context. Since dubs are also useful
for your demo reel, you may want to ask the producer
for one during your recording session. Realize, however,
that there is a cost involved. It doesn't hurt to offer to pay
for your dub.

If you have provided the voice-over for a video presentation or TV spot, the same editing and mixing process

takes place. Here, however the added dimension of visual images enters the picture.

The engineer and producer must put the audio elements *in sync* with the video elements. This process is called SWEETENING. A continuous flow of digital information called TIMECODE allows the video and audio machines to run in a synchronous mode which makes sure that when you see the bat hit the ball, you hear it as well. That's important. Our eye and ear coordination is so acute that we can perceive an out-of-sync discrepancy of 1/30th of a second.

All this post-production stuff is of little concern to most voice talent. It should be of interest, however, if only in understanding how the puzzle fits together. The professional expertise of each person in the process contributes something to the final product. A great spot owes its life to every member of the production team. So, by the way, does a bad spot.

A recording studio can be many things — old or new, bright or dreary, spacious or cramped. It may be a mom and pop operation or a large complex with many employees. You may find engraved coasters for your coffee mug or a sheep dog under the console. But no matter what it seems to be, what a recording studio really is is a miniature land of make-believe, unlike any other in the world. And with creative writers, talented voices, clever engineers, magical musicians and a zillion sound effects under one roof, the possibilities are endless.

CHAPTER 14

Dues and Don'ts

THE TALENT IN THE STUDIO was making his way
through a particularly difficult narration script when
he lost his place, causing his eye-to-mouth coordination
to falter, fumble and finally disintegrate before our ears.

"I'm sorry," he offered with a sheepish look over the
top of his copy stand, "but the typing fell off the page."

It was a funny reaction to his mistake and we all had a
good laugh. But face it, mistakes are bound to happen and
most of them are truly unimportant.

When you make an error, there's really nothing to be
gained by punishing yourself with lots of needless self-
deprecation. It's better to keep the mood of the session
positive, and just keep moving forward.

But while certain missteps can't be avoided, others can
be. So here's a review of some important do's and don'ts
we've covered so far, followed by some thoughts

concerning dues — that is, whether or not you should join the talent union.

THE VOICE-OVER CHECKLIST

1.   When you are called for a session, write down the *time, location, client, producer's name, type of work,* and *studio phone number.*

2.   Dress appropriately. Don't wear nylon clothing or anything that might create noise problems during the session.

3.   Always arrive at the studio about ten minutes before your session. The best excuse for being late is that you're dead.

4.   Avoid bringing children, family members or friends to a session without getting prior permission.

5.   Be rested and relaxed. Don't be on the run. It presents a bad image and affects your performance.

6.   Keep initial conversation positive. Don't come into a session complaining about your troubles or with lots of complaints. The producer/director wants to think you're excited about the project.

7.   Be ready to go to work. Don't spend a lot of time getting coffee or chatting with other studio personnel.

8.   Get your copy, discuss the approach with the director and go into the studio. Let the engineer know if you wish to sit or stand and whether you want headphones. Get comfortable. The microphone will be adjusted to you, not vice versa.

9.   Lay out the script so it can be easily seen and position it for minimum page turning.

10. Look for direction words in the copy and start making script notes.

11. Start warming up. Practice reading the copy as you plan to read it. Don't read to yourself. Practicing out loud lets the engineer set sound levels and gives the director a chance to make some early decisions before the tape starts rolling.

12. When tape is rolling (or the digital recorder is recording), you will get a vocal slate through the talkback. It will sound something like, "rolling on take five" or "this is spot two, take one." After you hear the talkback click off, take a moment to mentally focus and start reading. You don't usually need a visual signal to start. There is also no need for a vocal countdown.

13. While you're reading, keep movement to a minimum. You need to stay within the mike's pick-up pattern. Rustling clothing, chair shifting, tapping feet and jingling jewelry will all be picked up by the mike.

14. When the talkback is open (that is, being used), there is no need to speak louder. Just use your normal voice.

15. Avoid clearing your throat, coughing or sneezing directly into the microphone. A slight turn off-mike will be appreciated by those in the control room.

16. It often helps to have a little coffee, tea or even warm water at your side during the session. A dry mouth can be pretty noisy to a microphone only inches away. If you run out of liquid and need more, just ask.

17. Take direction respectfully. Always give the director the benefit of the doubt. If you have suggestions or

changes you'd like to make, wait a few takes. Ask the director if you can make suggestions. Don't arbitrarily make changes to the copy or concept, no matter how good you think they are. Also, you'll need to be prepared to have your ideas rejected.

18. Don't stop reading if you feel you've made a mistake. Often a mistake can be covered by a pick-up later. Follow the lead of your engineer and director. If they want you to stop, they will let you know.

19. If you have a false-start, wait for the engineer to slate a new take number. This helps a lot during the editing stage later.

20. Don't move the microphone or change your position after recording has begun. If you need to shift your position, ask the engineer to reset the mike.

21. Don't become worried about doing too many takes. It is normal to work a spot over and over. Some directors like to try to get the perfect read in a single take and will keep going until they hear it. Others like to concentrate on getting one line at a time and assembling the spot later. The adage is that you will do seven takes for every "director" in the control room. That means you're destined for fourteen at the very least. If you get out with less, consider yourself lucky. Twenty to thirty takes on one sixty-second radio spot is not unusual.

22. Listen carefully to playbacks. Use them as learning time, not as break time. If you want to hear a playback anytime during the session, ask your engineer.

23. If you need to take a break or refill your coffee cup, ask between takes. If you are uncomfortable, if the room

is too warm, if the lighting is bad or if you just need a breath of fresh air, tell the engineer. It's important that you feel good. At the same time, be careful not to become too demanding or hold up the session for extended periods.

24. Time is money in a studio and every project has a budget. Look to the engineer for session pacing. If you feel the engineer is trying to move the session along, try to keep pace. If the mood is relaxed with plenty of time for jokes and stories, feel free to join in and have fun.

25. Remember that everyone at the session is there for the same goal. Their positions, priorities and points of view may be different, but everyone wants a great spot when the session is over. It's not a competition. A group effort, using everyone's talents, will always produce the best results.

26. While you're working, any incoming telephone calls for you should be held at the reception desk. Don't have the session interrupted for your personal calls. If you have other business to take care of, do it after the session in another room.

27. Don't chew gum while recording. Believe it or not, some talent are guilty of this practice. Trying to stuff it in your cheek during the read doesn't work. Stuff it in the wastebasket instead.

28. When the session is over, wait to be excused from the booth. Pick up all your scripts and close the door behind you. You may wish to keep copies of the script for your personal files or for practice. Ask the producer.

29. Money matters are best left until after the session. If you are a union member and you have an agent, payment amounts should be very clear. Union members should

completely fill out a union contract, when required, at the end of the session and have it signed by the producer. You may also need to fill out a W4 form for tax purposes. In non-union situations, make sure it's clear who gets your bill and how much it will be. Also get any spot reference numbers and a signed purchase order if possible.

30. Check with the producer or director to see if you're free to leave. He or she may wish to hear a couple of takes played back before letting you go.

31. Try not to hang around after the session. There's all that post-production work that needs to be done. This is not the time for socializing. If you'd like to chat with the director, do it off the clock. Take a director to lunch.

32. Leave a copy of your demo tape if the director or studio doesn't have one.

33. Don't use the studio as a temporary office. Unless it's an emergency, make phone calls and take care of personal matters outside the studio. Don't tie up their business lines.

34. It's sometimes helpful if the studio knows where you are going when you leave. In the event of a script revision or equipment failure, they may need to find you quickly. Make sure your agent knows where you are at all times.

35. If you were pleased with your performance, ask for a dub of the completed spot. Some producers will even pay for it. Use it as a learning tool or as a sample for your demo tape.

36. A hardworking and considerate attitude on your part will make for happy directors, appreciative engineers and

delighted clients. Oh yes, and an invitation back for future work.

THERE'S ONE OTHER ASPECT of being a professional, and as you progress from job to job and from city to city, you'll eventually run into it.

There are two unions that govern performers: A.F.T.R.A. (American Federation of Television and Radio Artists) and S.A.G. (Screen Actors Guild). A.F.T.R.A. controls product recorded to tape or disc and S.A.G. controls product recorded to film. You may be required to join none, one or both of them depending on the market you're in and how often you're performing. These two unions will eventually merge but as of this writing they have not yet done so.

The unions negotiate contracts with area producers. These contracts set payment rates, payment schedules, working conditions, cycles of use for the commercials, health and retirement plans, and many rules and regulations governing both broadcast and non-broadcast use of voice talent. The producers who agree to abide by the union rules are called *signatories*. Talent agents who follow union guidelines become known as union *franchised*. Talent who pay the initiation fees and dues and adopt the contract become *members* of a national labor union and follow the same set of rules.

Are you ready for union membership? Well, if you're just starting your career, you have a little time to decide. If you live in a small town, the unions may not even be represented. But small towns tend to have very little work. If you go to cities where the work is, you'll probably find the unions.

Union membership has its pros and cons. In every market where the unions are present, there are non-union actors working on non-union jobs. In other words, they are working for producers who have not signed the union contract. Some producers will sign the contract and others won't.

To join or not to join is an important question, so here are some of the arguments to help you decide.

Bob, a non-union talent, is free to do what he wants. He can work for any non-signatory producer, in any studio, for whatever rate he can get. He can have anyone represent him. He doesn't have to do union paperwork, get authorization or waivers, worry about how and where his voice will be used, or pay union dues.

Sheila, a union talent, can only work for signatory producers. If she has representation, it must be by a franchised agent. She cannot work for less money than the union requires. The minimum union rate for a given job is known as "scale"; a union talent may work for over scale rates but never under scale without union authorization. In many cities, she must invoice the client using an A.F.T.R.A. form and note where the production is being used, when it will be used, how long it will be used, and the names of any other performers. She must pay an initiation fee to join, and yearly dues to remain a member in good standing.

At first glance, Bob seems to have it made. But Sheila has a few benefits to balance all the rules. The non-union talent may be able to set his own rate but his figure may be open to debate with the client. Since no contract is signed, the client may even come back to the non-union talent days later asking for, or demanding, a "better deal" on the rate. The union member has a fixed price for every job and it's not open to debate. The A.F.T.R.A. rate book, for instance, lists talent prices for everything from one radio spot running in Phoenix for three months to a video narration for lawn sprinklers that plays on machines in the home improvement departments of seven chain stores in Ohio. The signatory producer has already agreed to pay the going rate by signing the union contract and, where applicable, by signing the talent's invoice at the time of the session. The non-union talent is at the mercy of the producer's payment schedule while the union talent must be paid before a specified time or receive extra penalty fees from the producer. The union places restrictions on how long, how often and where the production can be used. The union talent may also receive fees called residuals. The non-union talent has no way of controlling these cycles of use and seldom gets residuals.

Signatories agree to pay social security matching fees for Sheila. They also agree to do all withholding for taxes so she doesn't end up with a huge tax bill at the end of the year. Bob must deal with taxes as well. Being non-union doesn't mean he's free from taxes.

The signatory producer is also charged a percentage of the talent's fee that goes into a health and retirement fund to benefit Sheila in years to come. Signatories agree to use only union talent in their productions. *Sigs* may hire Bob if it is his first union gig. However, to work for a signatory again after a thirty day period, Bob will have to join the union.

The union talent can qualify for medical benefits and a retirement plan. She can attend union meetings and conventions, run for board membership, be involved in contract negotiations and vote on union matters. Perhaps the most important aspect of union membership is the fact

that the union will back her up in a crisis. If a producer
refuses to pay, delays payment or violates use rules,
the union will come to Sheila's aid with phone calls, letters
or even legal assistance if necessary. Bob may be able
to make up his own rules, but he has no guarantee that
anyone else will play by them.

On the negative side, A.F.T.R.A. and S.A.G. locals can
charge a hefty initiation fee. It may take several paying
jobs just to cover the costs of joining. The dues are set by
your income level, but you still pay the minimum even
when you don't work. Every town has a fair number of
non-union producers. As a union member, you will not
be able to work for these people. Depending on the
strength of A.F.T.R.A. and S.A.G. in your area, the non-
union element may outnumber the union contingent. If
most of the work is going to non-union performers, you
will have a tough decision to make. You will have to
weigh the monetary costs against projected income and
the value of choice against the benefits of security. There
is also a provision in both unions for what is called
"financial core" status. This provision allows union
members to work both union and non-union gigs. It
comes with several restrictions, however, so check into it
fully before making any move to core status.

You cannot be forced to join the union. They can't even
solicit your membership until after you've worked on
your first union job. A decision one way or the other will
strongly affect your career, so do not take it lightly.

CHAPTER 15

Now You're Talking!

Do you have what it takes to be a voice star? You've read this book so now you know everything there is to know. Well, almost everything. Try reading the following tag:

The Winger Air Shuttle.
First to Salt Lake. Second to no one.

Now let's do a few takes with some one-word directions. This is going to take some fancy vocal footwork. There's no hurry, so take your time and think about subtle variations. All these direction words come from actual sessions but they're in no particular order. So if you're ready...

...we'll roll tape...

...this is "Winger Air" tag number 1...

...take number...

1. Hard Sell
2. Soft Sell
3. Testimonial
4. Humorous
5. Tired
6. Breathless
7. Conversational
8. Cartoon
9. Gravelly
10. Mellow
11. Technical
12. Dramatic
13. Poetic
14. Pitchman
15. Cute
16. Sincere
17. Tough
18. Inspirational
19. Squeaky
20. Lispy
21. Sexy
22. Ordinary
23. Amateur
24. Patriotic
25. Scared
26. Corny
27. Wicked
28. Dizzy
29. Youthful
30. Bright
31. Perky
32. Noisy
33. Milquetoast
34. Methodical
35. Newsperson
36. Heroic
37. Expectant
38. Rhythmic
39. Intimate
40. Hushed
41. Tight
42. Shy
43. Staccato
44. Hype
45. Authoritative
46. Amazed
47. Slow
48. Fast
49. Excited
50. Mumbled
51. Robotic
52. Energetic
53. Your way
54. Explanatory
55. Sly
56. High-brow
57. Sing-song
58. High
58b. The other High
59. Dull
60. Throaty
61. Babyish
62. Quaint
63. Elderly
64. Loud
65. Whispery
66. Tense
67. Announcer
68. Flat
69. Like a dog would read it
70. Like a cat would read it

Okay, I think we've got something to work with. Thanks a lot.

It's amazing when you think about all the potential styles of delivery and all the terms that can be used to direct you to a particular style. It's also pretty amazing that you can convey so many attitudes with your voice alone.

If you have the talent, you should treat it with respect. Don't sell yourself short. You possess a valuable ability that most people don't have. It seems to be such an easy career to anyone who hasn't actually pursued it. It isn't. Being a good voice-over actor is as hard as any job, with the added burden of trying to keep your ego afloat while outsiders punch holes in it. One of the most difficult challenges facing the actor is to accept that when someone says they don't like you, they are not talking about *you* personally. The same person who "can't stand you" for this project may "love you" for the next one.

There are a few producers out there who believe that for a few bucks actors can be compromised, abused and humiliated. Many auditions are known as "cattle calls" and the constant competition with your fellow performers can be frustrating. You may be able to complete your required job in fifteen minutes, but the effort you've invested leading up to that quarter hour may have taken years. No, it's not an easy job. It deserves proper consideration and compensation. You have to temper your self-pride so you don't become boorish, but you always need to keep a sense of value about yourself— not only to hold your body and soul together, but to bolster your self-confidence as you market yourself to the world.

It may be difficult building your voice career in a small town. The limited opportunities will inhibit your growth and earning potential. There is, however, no reason you can't start in a small town. Learning to read, act, react and self-promote is not a big city monopoly. If you plan to pursue this career any further, you'll need to keep moving to bigger and bigger cities until you reach your peak, or the end of your rope. A medium to large-size city can provide a comfortable living for the successful commercial voice actor. In this type of city you will find all the support services critical to success. You'll also find classes and workshops in commercial voice acting. If you want to learn about a city, ask people. Talk with production companies, advertising agencies, talent agents, recording studios, and other actors. For the most part, they're used to inquiries and no matter who you talk to, they're guaranteed to have an opinion about everyone else.

A certain stigma remains for some concerning the commercial actor. Some actors and producers see a dividing line between "serious" acting and the kind that's done in commercials. Some carry it as far as hanging a "sell-out" label on any performer who stoops so low as to work in an advertisement. Actually, it's a bit presumptuous to consider a commercial a lower form of theatrics, or to assume that, if he were alive today, Shakespeare wouldn't be an ad copywriter at J. Walter Thompson. The skills of characterization, attitude, focus, delivery, timing, control, and professionalism come into play just as much in commercial acting as they do in other forms. Plus, the commercial actor has the added concerns of working with time restraints. Any actor who can pull that off, in my view, deserves to be taken seriously.

Be aware that the business is cyclical and popularity tends to come and go. A talent who is overrun with work this quarter may be out of work next quarter. One of the main reasons for this is over-exposure. An actor may become so popular that his or her voice seems to be everywhere in the market. Too many producers start hearing it too often and suddenly they're on to somebody "new." There is also a tendency for local producers to want out-of-town voices in order to get a more unique sound. Ironically, many of these producers end up hiring some "hot" big city talent who's just as over-exposed on a national level.

It's often been said that these are the life stages of a professional commercial actor:

1. Who's Andy Freeze?
2. Get me Andy Freeze.
3. Get me an Andy Freeze type.
4. Get me a younger Andy Freeze.
5. Who's Andy Freeze?

Some commercial actors play from town to town like a traveling road show, staying until they get to step three above, then moving on. They're likely to pass through town again in a few years when producer and agency turnover will have made them a "new" talent again.

CHAPTER 16

The Future

O NE OF THE best things about voice-over is that you
can make it a life-long profession. It's hard to think
of another job that can keep you employed from
childhood through senior citizenship. As your voice
matures you will naturally gravitate from doing in-line
skate commercials to retirement home spots, but a well-
trained voice actor will usually enjoy a long career.

With advances in technology, several new areas are
opening up for talent. Voice-mail, automated ordering
systems, instructional videotapes, computer networks,
cable TV and infomercials are just some of the new arenas
requiring experienced voices.

Two of the most exciting are books-on-cassette and
interactive multi-media for computers. The former is
experiencing controlled growth while the latter appears
ready to explode.

Both abridged and unabridged audio versions of books are increasingly popular. Obviously, the rigors of reading an entire book aloud put this type of voice work in the domain of the hardy talent. If you've heard many books on cassette, you may have noticed a wide variety of presentation styles and degrees of quality. In most cases these tapes are produced under tight budgets and time constraints. The readers have to be very good so little editing will be needed. Sometimes the author of the work is requested to do the reading. A good author doesn't always make a good voice talent, however, so actors are often brought in to bring the work to life.

The actor may need to run the gamut of emotions, vary delivery styles and present a variety of character voices for dramatic fiction. On the other hand, non-fiction texts may require a controlled, authoritative style. Whatever the method, it's still an awful lot of reading. Even if the piece is recorded over several days, the actor needs a firm focus on the material and a good command of his or her vocal instrument.

Some people may view books-on-cassette as a poor substitute for honest reading, but in our rapidly moving society they offer an alternative for people wishing to keep up on issues or the latest popular novels. For the voice talent, they also provide a return to some of the better aspects of radio theater and storytelling. Right now, most of the work is produced in the major markets and is controlled by a small number of companies. But as competition and audience demand increases, we could see books on cassette become a strong and exciting medium for the voice actor.

Interactive multi-media is appearing everywhere. The

most obvious is in CD-ROM programs for business and home computers. Producers of everything from medical encyclopedias to home repair guides to invading-mutant-alien combat games are employing voice actors to fill a variety of roles. Interactive media is also appearing in museum exhibits, airports, and at numerous tourist attractions. The exciting aspects of this technology are based in the amazing storage capacity and speed of the compact disk or CD. At last count, a standard CD can store about 250,000 pages of printed material. It can also store drawings, diagrams, photographs, movies, sound effects, music and voices.

The interactive part of this format allows the user to make choices about how the information is presented. At several junctures along the program's path, the user is given the choice of taking two or more different paths.

In a standard audio/visual production the narrator or actor takes the audience from Point A to Point B in a straight line. The script has one beginning and one ending. This is known as a linear production.

TRADITIONAL LINEAR MEDIA

A ←——————————————————————→ B

In non-linear interactive media, however, there may be any number of starting points and multiple endings. The program may even be set up to return the user to alternate starting points, thus creating a show with no ending at all. Instead of one story to tell, the actor may have several. Whether this expanded format means certain talent will work more, or more talent will certainly work remains to

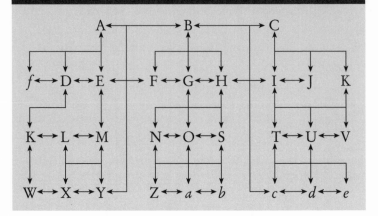

be seen. Either way, it could be a promising future for talent in interactive multi-media.

Well, this book is almost over and then you'll be on your own. If you're still unsure about your abilities, seek out a professional acting class. If available, find one that specializes in commercial voice acting.

You're entering a relatively small profession. Wanting to be a top voice talent is like wanting to be a first-chair violinist with a symphony orchestra. There are only a limited number of chairs available and the competition to sit down is formidable. On the other hand, somebody has to take a seat and it might as well be you. Acting in voice-overs is a wonderfully odd and irritatingly energizing profession where every job is a new experience and every session is an audition for the next.

So don't just stand there — start talking! Besides loving what you do, you may end up putting your mouth where the money is.

Glossary

AD AGENCY   A business that designs and produces advertising and public relations for other businesses. Advertising agencies are likely to be your main source of commercial voice work. They are usually founded on the concept of creativity, though some of them seem to have forgotten.

A.F.T.R.A.   The American Federation of Television and Radio Artists. A national labor union for commercial broadcast and "on air" talent. Some scripts may seem difficult until you read the A.F.T.R.A. contract.

ANNC: An abbreviation for announcer. Often used by copywriters.

AUDITION   A non-paying casting session at which several actors read for the same role to determine which one does the best job. Usually, the best actor is selected for the final production...usually.

BALLS   A deep and resonant vocal tone.

BED   The soundtrack that goes under your voice-over. It may be a bed of music or sound effects or a combination of both.

BILLBOARD   To emphasize or set apart a copy point is to *billboard* it.

BOOKING   A confirmed session. You got the job!

CANS   A hip term for headphones. Just imagine yourself making *spots* with *cans* on your ears.

CATTLE CALL   A term used to describe an audition where nearly every talent in town is invited. This situation is usually caused by a lack of specifics from the person doing the casting. They don't know what they want so they give everyone a chance to be heard. Or is that herd?

COLD READ   A reading done without any rehearsal.

COMML   Abbreviation for "commercial."

CONSOLE   The audio *board* or control panel that allows the engineer to direct the audio signal to the recorders, and to combine the various audio components into the final mix.

COPY   Another word for the "script."

COPY POINTS   The items in a script that require particular attention, and therefore particular interpretation by the voice actor.

CUE   Another term for the talkback system in a recording

studio. Cue is usually used in reference to the talkback used through headphones. It can also mean an audible or visual sign that tells you when to begin reading.

CUT & PASTE   The act of assembling parts from many takes into a composite. Until recently, this was all done manually by physically cutting the recording tape with a razor blade and splicing it together using a special adhesive tape. Today, this is often done on a computer but the term still applies.

DAT   Digital Audio Tape. A format that records sound digitally onto a small tape cartridge. A DAT is not much bigger than a matchbook but some can hold over two hours of sound.

DEMO   Short for *demonstration*, a demo can be a sample tape of a talent's voice used to show his or her abilities. It can also be an unpolished production of a spot used by an ad agency to sell a concept. In the construction trade, *demo* is an abbreviation for "demolition." Don't get the two confused.

DIGITAL RECORDING   A computer process by which sound is converted into a complex series of numbers and stored on recording tape, or in a computer hard drive.

DIRECTOR   The person in charge during the session. This person is often the copywriter as well.

DONUT   A type of spot that has prerecorded material at the beginning and at the end with a "hole" in the middle for the voice part. The parts can be reversed as well, with the voice being the donut and the pre-recorded stuff in the hole.

DUB   An audio or video copy. Also called a *dupe* (short for duplicate).

EDITING   The cutting and rearranging of selected audio parts into a composite take. Also the removal of extraneous sounds from an audio track. Editing can be accomplished by physically cutting the tape or by electronic means. The point at which two parts are joined is called a *splice*.

ELLIPSIS   A favorite form of punctuation for many copywriters. It's those…well…you know…those three periods in a row that usually signify a thoughtful pause in your delivery.

ENGINEER   The technical person who runs all the equipment in the studio. A person who believes editing is the splice of life.

FALSE START   Term used to describe a take in which the talent makes an error within the first couple of lines. The take is usually stopped, and a new take is slated.

FRANCHISED   Term applied to talent agents who have adopted the guidelines of A.F.T.R.A. If a union talent has an agent, it must be a franchised agent.

FREELANCE   A *freelance* talent is one who works for many different employers and is free to pursue work from several sources. By the way, the term comes from the name applied to knights who offered their services to any commander. Along those lines, today's talent would love to freelance-a-lot.

Glossary

GIG   A job. A performance. The recording session. A "sig gig" is a union job.

GOOD PIPES   A talent with *good pipes* has vocal strength, authority and a deep rich quality.

HEADS OUT   Tape wound on a reel so that the beginning of the sound is on the outside. Usually marked with red adhesive tape. See *tails out*.

HIGH-SPEED DUB   A tape copy that is made at several times normal speed. Often used in reference to tape duplication. High speed dubs are often less costly and have a quicker turnaround time than *real time* or *at speed* dubs. They can be susceptible to problems, so always check your dubs before releasing them to prospective clients.

HOOK   The grabber. The point in the spot where the content or delivery makes a special connection with the listener. It's the thing that makes the spot work.

HOT MIKE   A microphone that is turned on.

HOUSE TAPE   A voice demo tape that includes short samples of all talent represented by a certain agent. Not something you use to seal cracks in walls.

IN-HOUSE   A production produced for the client in the client's own facilities. A project produced in-house is not sent to outside contractors for production. Employees of the client may write, produce, direct, engineer and star in these productions. Some larger corporations have very fine in-house production departments producing corporate training, promotion and sales pieces.

INSERT   A form of pick-up where a short segment of the script is reread from one point to another.

IN THE CAN   A phase borrowed from the film business. When a good take is achieved, it is considered ready for processing or *in the can*. It generally means that the director has the take he wants. It's been suggested that this phrase can also refer to where the talent is when the director needs him most.

J-CARD   A paper label for audio cassette boxes. It has a "J" shape when folded.

LAUNDRY LIST   A long series of copy points in a script. The object for the talent is to read the points with varying emphasis so they don't sound like a list.

LAY IT DOWN   See *record it*.

LOOPING   Replacing a voice track that is in sync with the picture when the original track cannot be used. This is a form of lip-syncing in which the talent watches a scene over and over while recording a new soundtrack until it perfectly matches the picture.

MAJOR MARKETS   Unionspeak for the three major voice markets of New York, Chicago and Los Angeles, where most voice talent can make the biggest bucks if they're good enough.

MASTER   The original recording. The tape from which dubs are made. Also a machine that controls other machines in the studio.

MIX   The final audio product combining all the elements into one composite soundtrack. *Mix* also applies to the act of creating the mix. This is sometimes referred to as the *mixdown*. Mixed up yet?

MOUTH NOISE   Also known as *clicks & pops*. A dry mouth produces much more mouth noise than a damp one. Cigarette smoking also contributes to a dry mouth. The less mouth noise you have, the less editing has to be done later. This saves the producer money which makes the client happy.

OFF-CAMERA   A part for which you supply only your voice to a TV spot or video presentation.

ON-CAMERA   A part in a TV spot or video production where you actually appear on screen. It pays more than an off-camera voice-over, but often requires more work. And much more make-up.

PAYMASTER   A payroll service that handles talent pay- ments for the producer. Paymasters usually compute all the necessary withholdings for taxes, FICA, etc., and many issue reuse notices to the producer when a spot has reached its expiration date. Anyone with "pay" in their name can't be all bad.

PHONE PATCH   This sounds like something you would put on a broken phone, but it's actually a session where the talent and the director are in separate locations. The session must be "patched" over telephone lines so everyone can hear everyone else.

PICK-UP   To start reading the script from a place other than the beginning. A *pick-up* is usually required when the top part of the script has been successfully completed and only the end needs to be worked on. Narration scripts are usually done in a series of pick-ups. Pick-up can also be a request to read faster ("Let's pick it up!") In fact, you may even be requested to pick up your pick-up.

POST   A short form of *post production*. This is the term applied to all the work that goes into a production after the talent leaves. This includes such processes as editing, multi-tracking, music selection, adding special effects and mixing.

PRODUCER   The person who organizes the session and makes sure it stays on budget. Also, the person most likely to be on the phone during the session.

PROTECTION   You may be asked to "do another take for protection." This means that you have given the director a take she likes but she wants you to do it again to make sure it was the best. Also referred to as "insurance."

RECORD IT   See *lay it down*.

RED LIGHT IT   See *record it*.

RESIDUALS   If a broadcast spot is used past its expiration date, the talent is entitled to residual or "reuse" payments that extend the spot's cycle of use. Usually, these use cycles are broken down into thirteen week periods. Sometimes the talent makes more money in residual payments than in the initial session.

REVERB   Another term for echo. Different types and amounts of reverb are sometimes added to your voice to place you in a certain environment, or to add an other-worldly sound to your voice. There's also a certain type of reverb called "delay" that repeats sounds back to you repeats sounds back to you repeats sounds back to you.

ROOMTONE   The sound a room makes without anyone in it. Every room has a different sound, so recording in the same room is sometimes critical when trying to match voice parts from one session to another.

S.A.G.   Screen Actors Guild. The labor union that oversees performers whose work is recorded to a film medium.

SCALE   Nothing fishy about this, it's the absolute minimum payment a union voice talent will work for on a given project.

SCRIPT   The words you read. The written version of the spot. Often written by one person and rewritten by everyone else.

SESSION   The event at which talent performs the script for recording purposes.

SFX   Abbreviation for *sound effects*. Sometimes also written as EFX or simply FX.

SIBILANCE   A drawn out or excessive "S" sound during speech. In extreme cases, the "S" sound is accompanied by a whistle. Sibilance is annoying and a hindrance to some voice actors. "S" is a popular letter with copywriters. It can be tough to find a line without any in it. Except that last one.

SIGNATORY   A producer who has signed the A.F.T.R.A. union contract and agrees to observe its rates and guidelines. Also called a *sig* by people who prefer one syllable words.

SLATE   An audible announcement of the take number recorded ahead of your read. The slate aids the engineer in finding the favorite takes for editing.

SPEC   Short for *speculative*. It usually means volunteering your services and postponing payment until a project sells. The best definition of *spec* ever heard is "working for nothing now on the promise of getting more than you deserve later on."

SPOT   A commercial for radio or television. When you're booked for a job, you're on the spot in more ways than one.

STUDIO   The room in which you'll do most of your work. An audio isolation room where the talent performs, usually paired with the control room. If you've ever worked in some of the small ones, you'll know why they're sometimes called the *booth*.

TAG   A short portion of a spot, usually placed at the end. A tag may say something such as, "Available at all Price-Mart Stores through Friday." Tags are often delivered by a voice talent different from those in the main body of the ad.

TAILS OUT   Recording tape wound on a reel so that the end of the soundtrack is on the outside. A tape wound *tails out* is usually marked with blue adhesive tape, while one wound *heads out* is usually marked with red adhesive tape. Remember "redheads and blue-tail flies."

TAKES   Each reading of the copy is called a *take*. They are consecutively numbered and logged. During a session, a frustrated talent once apologized for doing too many takes. "Don't worry about it," said the engineer, "I've got plenty of numbers left."

TALENT AGENT   Person whose firm serves as an actor's representative. The producer seeking talent often calls the talent agent to arrange scheduling, organize auditions, get demo tapes and find out how much it will cost to cast. Agents usually represent a pool of talent who work in many aspects of the commercial biz, including voice-over. Your opinion of your agent is likely to change daily.

TALKBACK   The system that allows people in the control room to talk with the talent in the studio.

VOICE-OVER   The act of providing one's voice to a media project. Called voice-over because the voice is usually mixed over the top of music and sound effects. Actually, even a voice mixed underneath is still called a voice-over.

WALLA   The sound of many voices talking at once, such as at a party or in a restaurant. Also known as "walla walla," this old sound effects term is derived from the idea that if a group of people got together and just kept saying *walla* over and over, it would create a good sound ambiance for a crowded scene. It really works. Try it. Do some vocal acting with lots of emotion while only saying *walla*.

WET   A voice or sound with reverb added to it.

WILD LINE   A single line from the script that is reread several times in succession until the perfect read is achieved. Wild lines are often done in a series. The slate may say something such as, "This is wild line pick-up take twelve A, B & C." This means you will read the line three times on this slate without interruption by the director. It is considered "wild" because it is done separately from the entire script. In video or film work, they are lines that occur when the camera is on something other than you. They are "wild" because it is not necessary for them to be in sync with your mouth.

WINDSCREEN   A foam cover or fabric guard placed over a microphone to help prevent popped "P's" and other plosive sounds. Sometimes called a "windsock" or "pop filter."

WOODSHED   To rehearse or practice reading copy out loud. This term is said to come from old theater days when actors would have to rehearse out in the woodshed before going into the theater to perform.

WORKSTATION   The term used to describe several types of digital audio production computers. They manipulate audio in the digital realm, and many engineers consider them playstations as well.

Okay, now go back to page one and read this book aloud.

Index

ABOUT THE AUTHOR

As a recording studio sound designer, Chris Douthitt has worked with much of our country's finest voice talent for over twenty years.

He's recorded everyone from Hollywood legends to nervous first-timers. He's also written, produced, directed and acted in many commercials himself, getting a look at the process from every perspective.

By regular involvement in voice workshops and classes, Chris has helped hundreds of newcomers get started in the business.

He, his wife Carol and 5 cats live on Whidbey Island in Washington.

ABOUT THE EDITOR

When he's not working on projects like this book, Tom Wiecks writes and produces commercials.

His ads have won recognition from The One Show, the New York Art Directors' Club, the Hollywood Radio and Television Society, the Clio awards and others.

He heads Wiecks & Associates, Inc., a Portland, Oregon creative services company.

We can't help you succeed in voice-overs
unless you speak up.

1-800-557-3378

WELCOME to the Creative Dept. catalog, a resource set up by and for voice-over people. We're here to help you expand your creative abilities and become the best voice talent you can be.

What few good books and tapes that exist on the subject have sometimes been hard to find. Now they're as easy as calling 1-800-557-3378.

So here's wishing you all the best, and we hope you'll share your comments and suggestions. Let us hear that voice of yours.

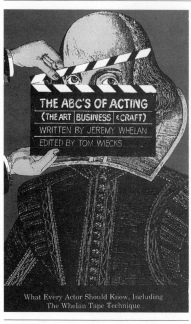

THE ABC'S OF ACTING
(THE ART BUSINESS & CRAFT)
WRITTEN BY JEREMY WHELAN
EDITED BY TOM WIECKS

What Every Actor Should Know, Including
The Whelan Tape Technique

"...helpful in bringing the necessary battle between instinct and technique to a peaceful accord."
—KELSEY GRAMMER, star of Cheers and Frasier

"Full of innovative techniques and sound advice, all presented in a straightforward style that reflects a real love of acting. A book any actor could learn something from."
—ENTERTAINMENT REVUE

The ABC's of Acting

BY JEREMY WHELAN

THE FIRST STEP in becoming a better voice talent might well be becoming a better actor. *The ABC's of Acting*, called "a first class primer for the actor...precise, sharp and amazingly compact"can help.

Whelan is a 30-year veteran of stage and screen who wrote this book for acting workshops he's conducted on both coasts. In easily understood terms, he covers the basics every actor should know, including his own innovative Whelan Tape Technique.

See why your voice is one of the only two acting tools you have. Learn how performing for the camera is different from performing on stage. Understand the power of changing your voice. Have an on-location movie crew explain the filming process to you. Selected by the Fireside Theatre Book Club — as well as by hundreds of college acting teachers and bookstores coast to coast — this book can help you become a better actor.

to order anytime, call
1-800-557-3378

ISBN 0-935566-26-0, 160 pages, Paper, $10.95 + shipping & handling

Voice-Overs: Putting Your Mouth Where the Money Is

BY CHRIS DOUTHITT

PERHAPS THE MOST complete overview yet of the voice-over business, this book explains more than just the voice talent's job. It helps you understand the whole production process and what's expected of you by the writer, engineer, ad agency, agent, talent union—and, of course, the client.

Douthitt is a veteran recording studio sound designer who's also a writer, director, producer and voice talent himself. He thinks the best place to start a voice-over career is wherever you happen to be now, and he details how to do it.

Learn all about interpreting scripts and taking direction. Preparing your demo tape. What happens during recording sessions. How voice casting works. Exactly how much voice-overs pay. And much, much more.

Complete with over 20 pages of sample radio, TV, narration and animation scripts, this is one book that has people talking.

"Damn good book—the most comprehensive and practical primer on the subject that we've ever seen. Thousands of very talented voices traipse through our lobby each year. Most of them would benefit considerably by studying Douthitt's how-to-do-it-right approach."
— BOB LLOYD,
owner of *The VoiceCaster*,
Burbank's voice casting specialists

"There can never be enough information about the dynamic, ever-growing voice-over industry. That's why I welcome Voice-Overs: Putting Your Mouth Where the Money Is *as a worthwhile new addition. Enjoy!"*
— SUSAN BLU,
animation director, voice-over artist and co-author of
Word of Mouth: A Guide to Voice-Over Excellence

to order anytime, call
1-800-557-3378

ISBN 0-935566-21-X
240 pages
Paper
$19.95 + shipping & handling

Word of Mouth: A Guide to Commercial Voice-Over Excellence

(The Audio Cassette)

BY SUSAN BLU
and MOLLY ANN MULLIN

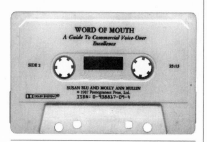

THIS IS THE audio cassette produced to accompany the *Word of Mouth* book on the next page.

It's not just voices reading the book. The authors and other actors present a series of skits that help amplify the book's main points.

It's a big help hearing examples of recommended warm-up exercises, for example, or "making your voice come from different parts of your body."

You'll also hear "The Basic Process" of copy interpretation demonstrated. Check out a professional-sounding demo tape. Overhear what goes on at a casting session. Even listen in on an all-too-real scene: a voice talent struggling to stay positive while chaotic clients in the control room keep rewriting her script.

Word of Mouth, the book, makes even more sense with *Word of Mouth*, the tape.

ISBN 0-938817-09-4
51 minutes
Cassette
$11.95 + shipping & handling

to order anytime, call
the creative dept.
1-800-557-3378

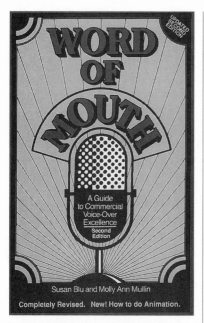

"This book is pure gold, not just for anyone in the voice-over business — it gives all of us in the acting game a fresh look at ourselves."
—BETTY WHITE

"If he'd read, studied and used this excellent guide, Quasimodo would have kissed bell-ringing goodbye. I strongly recommend it."
—EDWARD ASNER

Word of Mouth: A Guide to Commercial Voice-Over Excellence

BY SUSAN BLU
and MOLLY ANN MULLIN

ONE OF THE BEST-READ books in the voice-over industry, *Word of Mouth* explains everything you need to know to do effective voice-overs and find jobs in this growing field.

First published in 1987, it's been completely revised recently and now includes information on how to do animation voice-overs as well.

Susan Blu is not only a leading national voice talent and a writer, but an animation director and voice-over teacher, too. When Molly Ann Mullin isn't doing voice-overs , she's writing plays for radio, TV and the stage.

Together they pass along a rich collection of specific tips and techniques, from loosening-up exercises to their "Basic Process" for interpreting copy.

Equally valuable are the listings in the back of the book: telephone numbers for voice-over workshops in various cities around the country, sources to help you produce your demo tapes, even names and numbers of voice-over agents in major cities.

ISBN 0-938817-32-9
160 pages
Paper
$11.95 + shipping & handling

to order anytime, call
1-800-557-3378

How to Read Copy

BY ADRIAN CRONAUER

REMEMBER THE MOVIE *Good Morning, Vietnam?* Robin Williams starred in it as real life Armed Forces radio personality Adrian Cronauer. More recently, Cronauer's written this book passing along what he's learned about voice-overs after years on the air and teaching voice-over classes.

As the liner notes say, when you've finished it "you probably won't *have* all the skills needed to compete with professional voice-overs; that takes months, even years of practice. But you'll know what those skills *are* and when you do practice you'll know what you should by doing."

Cronauer focuses on common mistakes that separate amateurs and pros. Words to stress and not to stress. Tips on working in recording studios. Effective ways to market yourself. There's even a free audio cassette that comes with the book, with the author demonstrating important points.

If you want to know how to read copy, read *"How to Read Copy"*.

ISBN 0-929387-14-7
208 pages
Cloth
$29.95 + shipping & handling

Order Form

to order by phone:	Call toll free 1-800-557-3378, anytime. Please have your Visa or MasterCard ready.
to order by fax:	Call (503) 294-7973, anytime.
to order by mail:	Creative Dept. P.O. Box 69552 Portland, Oregon 97201

Please send me the following books or tapes. I understand I may return any unread book in its original condition for a refund within 15 days, but that audio cassettes may not be returned, and you cannot refund shipping costs.

QTY	TITLE	PRICE	TOTAL
_____	The ABC's of Acting: The Art, Business & Craft	$ 10.95	
_____	Voice-Overs: Putting Your Mouth Where the Money Is	$ 19.95	
_____	Word of Mouth: A Guide to Voice-Over Excellence (*cassette*)	$ 11.95	
_____	Word of Mouth: A Guide to Voice-Over Excellence (*book*)	$ 11.95	
_____	How To Read Copy (*hardcover book & free cassette*)	$ 29.95	
_____	Total items ordered	*subtotal:* $	

Add shipping & handling
AIR MAIL: *$3.95 per item*
BOOK RATE: (*allow 3 to 4 weeks*):
$2 for 1st item, $1 for each additional item $

☐ *check or money order enclosed*
☐ *bill my:* ○ Visa ○ MasterCard

total order: $

NUMBER _____   EXPIRES _____

NAME _____   SIGNATURE _____

ADDRESS _____   CITY _____   STATE ____   ZIP ____

DAYTIME PHONE _____

Order Form

to order by phone:	Call toll free 1-800-557-3378, anytime. Please have your Visa or MasterCard ready.
to order by fax:	Call (503) 294-7973, anytime.
to order by mail:	Creative Dept. P.O. Box 69552 Portland, Oregon 97201

Please send me the following books or tapes. I understand I may return any unread book in its original condition for a refund within 15 days, but that audio cassettes may not be returned, and you cannot refund shipping costs.

QTY	TITLE	PRICE	TOTAL
	The ABC's of Acting: The Art, Business & Craft	$ 10.95	
	Voice-Overs: Putting Your Mouth Where the Money Is	$ 19.95	
	Word of Mouth: A Guide to Voice-Over Excellence (*cassette*)	$ 11.95	
	Word of Mouth: A Guide to Voice-Over Excellence (*book*)	$ 11.95	
	How To Read Copy (*hardcover book & free cassette*)	$ 29.95	
	Total items ordered	*subtotal:* $	

Add shipping & handling
AIR MAIL: *$3.95 per item*
BOOK RATE: (*allow 3 to 4 weeks*):
$2 for 1st item, $1 for each additional item $

☐ *check or money order enclosed*
☐ *bill my:* ○ Visa ○ MasterCard

total order: $

NUMBER

EXPIRES

NAME

SIGNATURE

ADDRESS

CITY   STATE   ZIP

DAYTIME PHONE